On the Cyber

Sean Swan (Editor)

ISBN 978-1-105-70991-3

Table of Contents

Introduction	Sean Swan	6
Pirates of the Political Realm	Daniel Bossier	8
SOPA: An Objective Point of View	Evan Bull	13
Pirate Party Politics: An understanding of the culture supporting the party and a contextualization of its political successes	Alexandra Catibayan	18
Intellectual Property and Piracy	Kieran Craigie	22
From Sweden to Tunisia: The Development of the Pirate Party	Alexis DiSanza	26
Cyber Warfare: The Stuxnet Virus and its Implications for Interstate Conflicts	John Emery	31
Culture Conflict	Yvonne Gay	38
Wikileaks and Free Speech	Nicholas Halliburton	42
Free Speech	Hannah Hawkings	51
Freedom of Speech on the Internet; The Role of the Internet in the Middle East Uprisings	Joshua Kellems	57
From Citizen to Suspect: Freedom of Speech and the Patriot Act	John Mallahan	61
Anonymous: The Social Organism	Dustin Phillips	67
Identifying Anonymous	Jacqueline Pittaway	73
Anonymous is Not One Person	Richard Redford	79
Legal Responses to Anonymous	Austin Rogers	83
The Ethics of Copyright in the Digital Age	Cory Stumpf	87
Copyright and The Music Industry	Ryan Thompson	92
Copyright and U.S. Relations	Benjamin Tibbs	96
Kopimism: A New Religion	Emma Wabunsee-Kelly	102
Digitalization and the Limits of Copyright Law	Koby Warren	107
Afterword: On the Pirate Party	Rick Falkvinge	113

Introduction

Sean Swan

This book is essentially a pedagogical device – as much sofor the authors as for the reader. It consists of a series of presentation papers written by students in a course I taught at Gonzaga University in the spring semester of 2012. The course was entitled 'Cyber Politics' and was a broad sweep through the various ways in which digitalization has impacted the political realm from the Arab Spring and WikiLeaks to cyber war and the Pirate Party. The bulk of the papers contained in this volume were presented at the 10th Annual *Spokane Intercollegiate Research* Conference (SIRC) held on April 21, 2012, at Gonzaga University

One of the main implications of digitalization is the flattening of hierarchies. Previously the gulf separating nuclear from non-nuclear states and separating the state from the individual was huge. In the cyber realm this hierarchy has been flattened, if not inverted. Previously the only way for musicians to reach an audience was via the record 'industry' which acted as a musical gatekeeper, choosing what choice of music the public would have. This is no longer the case today. It is open to anybody to 'broadcast' themselves via YouTube and to make their music available as mp3 downloads. This, in and of itself, does not earn money for the musicians in question, but it can serve as excellent advertising/publicity which can be turned into income via live performances. Two obvious examples would be the South African group *Die Antwoord* or English punk poet *Attila the Stockbroker.*

Of course such 'do-it-yourself' activity offers nothing to third parties such as record labels. It is thus hardly surprising that they, and Hollywood, have been some of the most vociferous critics of file-sharing. In the world of academic publication all the financial benefit accrues to the 'third party' – the publisher. It was thus interesting recently to read that:

> Exasperated by rising subscription costs charged by academic publishers, Harvard University has encouraged its faculty members to make their research freely available through open access journals and to resign from publications that keep articles behind paywalls.
>
> (Ian Sample, 'Harvard University says it can't afford journal publishers' prices' guardian.co.uk, Tuesday 24 April 2012)

This challenging of traditional gatekeepers is a tendency which is likely to continue. For some, this conjures forth a vision of anarchy in which everything and anything will be published without the quality control of a 'gatekeeper'. How will we be able to tell the gold from the dross? There are two possible responses to this. The blunt and simple answer is you will have to be your own gate-keeper. You will have to think for yourself. A second answer is that quality control will arise from the swarm. If you want to purchase a book on Amazon, you can read the reviews written by others who have already read the book. These reviews are themselves ranked in terms of 'usefulness' and, like the reviews, are produced by the 'swarm'. That is, they are produced by the individual, unpaid and voluntary, initiative of those who are interested in the book in question. Other examples of the manner in which the 'swarm' performs the roles traditionally performed by gatekeepers include Wikipedia and the way in which comments are made, and rated, on online newspapers articles.

How can one best demonstrate to a class of undergraduates the manner in which digitalization empowers the individual? How it allows everybody to be their own publisher? Well, this book is an attempt to do exactly that. This is a book without a publisher.

I would like to thank Rick Falkvinge, founder of *Piratpartiet*, the Swedish Pirate Party, which was the original pirate party, for agreeing to contribute an article to this book. It was especially appreciated given the time constraints involved and the fact that he was forced to write most of it while on board a plane!

Thanks also to Bethany Blair (BB) for technical assistance.

Finally, the views expressed herein represent the opinions of the authors severally. They do not necessarily all share the views expressed by other authors in this book. Nor should this book, or any author in it, be understood as representing the views of Gonzaga University, the Political Science Department of Gonzaga University or anything or anybody beyond themselves. Their voices are their own.

swan@gonzaga.edu

Pirates of the Political Realm

Daniel Bossier

Over the last six years the pirate party has transitioned from an upstart and somewhat tongue in cheek founding to becoming an international political influence. The pirate party was originally founded in Sweden in January of 2006 by Rick Falkvinge who had previously been an IT under the partial influence of the Piratebyrån (a Swedish organization formed in order to combat the anti-pirate bureau). Falkvinge was motivated to quit his job and enter into the political realm when in 2005 he became concerned with three issues: patent monopolies on software, copyright monopoly harshening and data retention direction (using mobile phones as government tracking devices). Surprisingly to Falkvinge, the party achieved significant and immediate success by achieving 0.63% of the vote in the Swedish elections that was held a mere nine mounts after the party was founded. Although this number may appear minute, it was still enough to rank as the 10th most popular party in Sweden.

Following the 2006 election, Falkvinge developed a five step plan for the party. To become the most popular party amongst young voters, to achieve at least 4% in a European election, gaining representation in the Swedish Parliament, earn at least 5% of the vote in 3-4 other countries and subsequently seeing the global significance of the pirate party. Three and a half years after this plan, there was a breakthrough in the expanded success of the party. In 2009 Pirate Party International (whose purpose is, "to help establish, to support and promote, and to maintain communication and co-operation between pirate parties around the world") held a conference in Uppsala, Sweden where pirate parties from a number of different countries met in order to establish unifying policy agreements amongst the different policies. There were three central issues that were ultimately agreed upon. First: reform of copyright, exemption of non-commercial activity from copyright regulation, reduction of the duration of copyright protections (no more than 5 years in length); banning of DRM technologies, opposition to media or hardware levies. Second: reform of patent law, particularly stating that patents on life (including patents on seeds and on genes) and software should not be allowed. Lastly: strengthening civil rights, transparent government, speedy and fair trial and freedom of speech; expansion of the right to anonymity in communication. This agreement became known as the Uppsala Declaration. The same year as the Uppsala Declaration, the pirate party saw an incredible spike in both interest and support. In 2009 the Pirate Party received 7.3% of the vote, 2 seats in the European Parliamentary election and also held 25% of the vote of those under the age of 30. This success fulfilled the first two of the parties five year plan.

Although the party was unable to acquire seats in Sweden's government it was able to take 2 out of the 20 available seats in the European parliament. Falkvinge cites the failure to acquire representation within the Swedish Parliament on the lack of an established party platform fit for an elected official. In order to remedy this Falkvinge claims that there will be a fully comprised platform prior to the 2014 Swedish elections. However, despite the fact that the third point on the party's five year plan was not achieved, its significant success in Germany and in the European parliament further illustrates the progression of the pirate party. In the 2011 Berlin state election, the pirate party received 8.9% of the votes and managed for the first time to overcome the 5% threshold and to win seats (15 of the 141) in the German state parliament with all 15 of the Pirate Party candidates being elected.

Current Status:

These are the primary illustrations of the rapid expansion and success that the pirate party has seen since its founding. The party is rapidly becoming a significant force on the international political stage. Currently there are Pirate Parties in 56 different countries including 2 Seats in the European Parliament, 15 seats in the Berlin Parliament as well as 150+ seats in local councils. Additionally, the popularity of this party has not ceased. As recently as April 9th the pirate party is polling at 13% in Germany, according to the Forsa Institute.

In this success, Rick Falkvinge stepped down from Swedish Pirate Party Leader on January 1st, 2011, succeeded by Anna Troberg, and is currently a self titled political evangelist who is working to continue the awareness and success of international pirate parties. Since he has stepped down, Rick Falkvinge has posted on his personal website a list of the pirate party's principles and philosophy.

The principles and philosophy of the pirate party as constructed by Rick Falkvinge are empowerment, privacy, transparency, ticks (tools, ideas, culture, knowledge and sentiments), humanism, diversity, resilience, swarm economy and quality legislation. These principles primarily have to do with the protection of individual rights and liberties and ensuring a government that is reactive as opposed to proactive. Upon analyzing the principles and philosophy that Falkvinge had laid out I began to compare them to other established political parties and found striking similarities between the pirate party and the libertarian party.

According to the libertarian party website, the libertarian party platform consists of 27 categories or principles and these principles are essentially extensions or expansions upon the philosophy of the pirate party. As expected, the issues that the libertarian party is concerned with pertain to the protection of the liberties of the individual and the limiting of the government so that it only performs necessary functions. For example, the first four points of the libertarian party platform are all entirely agreed upon by the pirate party. They are personal liberty, expression and communication, personal privacy, and personal relationships. Upon further examination, it seems that the only issue that the pirate party and the libertarian party could potentially disagree on is the issues of property and contract. The pirate party is of course supportive of digital file sharing, and inherently opposed to the formulation of patents as well as the limiting of copyrights. On the topic of file sharing, Rick Falkvinge has stated that, "It's not theft. It's an infringement on a monopoly. If it was theft and it was property, we wouldn't need a copyright law, ordinary property laws would suffice." Falkvinge is making a distinction between theft and copying, for when theft occurs the original copy or document is removed from one person and granted access to by another. Copying or downloading on the other hand allows both individuals access to the same information. One person's data or information has been expanded and the other individual's has remained the same. On the other hand, the libertarian party's stance on property and contract is as follows: "Property rights are entitled to the same protection as all other human rights. The owners of property have the full right to control, use, dispose of, or in any manner enjoy, their property without interference, until and unless the exercise of their control infringes the valid rights of others. We oppose all controls on wages, prices, rents, profits, production, and interest rates. We advocate the repeal of all laws banning or restricting the advertising of prices, products, or services. We oppose all violations of the right to private property, liberty of contract, and freedom of trade." If libertarians do not accept the stance on information sharing and piracy that Falkvinge does, then there could clearly be a potential issue.

Although there are potential topics of contention between the pirate party and the libertarian party, it is indubitably clear that the pirate party is essentially a libertarian movement. The party is pro individual rights and not definitively aligned with left or ring wing political viewpoints. In order to get a closer understanding of the party's political leanings I chose to compare the pirate party to other famous libertarian movements, the recent tea party movement and the yippie/hippie movement of the late 1960s.

The tea party movement first began in 2009 and strongly called for economic reform. Primarily the tea party sought reductions in government spending, tax cuts and the less regulations over the American free market. Additionally, tea party advocates where much more united in their political alignment as they identified themselves as conservative- libertarian and predominantly consisted of married, Anglo-Saxons of an above average age. In addition to the differences in the demographics (the pirate party being overwhelmingly comprised of young males) of each of these political movements the two also are not entirely in agreement on their focus. The pirate party also appears to be more concerned with social and internet liberties as opposed to economic reforms. From this it can be discerned that the pirate party is not radically right and perhaps not even predominantly conservative, in order to determine if they are in fact a more leftist movement I chose to compare the party to the radical leftist libertarian affiliation known as the yippies.

The YIPs or the youth international party was co-founded in 1967 by Abbie Hoffman, the famous political and social activists. The group was notable for being an organized manifestation of the hippy ideal while remaining free of any sort of hierarchy or leaders. It is with respects to the organization of the movement as well as the fact that the yippies was comprised almost exclusively by the youth that similarities can be seen with the pirate party. In fact, Rick Falkvinge drew his own connection between the hippie movements and the pirate party. In his "I am a Pirate" Ted Talk Falkvinge mentions that the primary concerns for 17 year olds in the 1960s and 70s was the freedom of peace and love. Today, the primary concern of this same age group is freedom of speech and openness and most notably how these issues pertain to the internet. Furthermore, as with the yippies, the pirate party is a decentralized affiliation with no dogmatic doctrine or definitive leader. Falkvinge makes it clear that he is not the ultimate controller of this ideal, as some have accused Julian Assange of Wikileaks fame of being, as he is quick to admit his own faults and attempts to ensure that the actions behind the pirate party are the consensus of its members. Additionally, the yippies were primarily concerned with creating equality including the rights and freedom of information for all that the pirates approve of. The only thing that clearly indicates that the pirate party is not as left wing as the yippies were is that pirates have sought to convey their opinions through the current political system as opposed to going outside of the system. Abbie Hoffman stated, "We shall not defeat America by organizing a political party. We shall do it by building a new nation – a nation as rugged as the marijuana leaf." The pirate party is not so left that it could be labeled entirely anarchistic but instead seeks the insurance of freedom and liberty on the internet and with information.

Through an analysis of the pirate party's principles and philosophy and comparisons to other political movements it is clear that the party is essentially a rebranding of a moderately left libertarian ideal and harnessing the current concerns that today's technologically aware have over the internet. Although the party is not altogether unique as it clearly holds a consistency with libertarian ideals it is the first party that has successfully captured the concerns of the internet and attempted to ensure that the ideals that people have become accustomed to as well as developed remain intact.

Works Cited

"European Pirate Platform 2009." *Piratpartiet*. Web. Apr. 2012. <http://www.piratpartiet.se/nyheter/european_pirate_platform_2009>.

Falkvinge, Rick. "Rick Falkvinge: I Am a Pirate." *TED: Ideas worth Spreading.* TED, Apr. 2012. Web. Apr. 2012. <http://www.ted.com/talks/rick_falkvinge_i_am_a_pirate.html>.

Falkvinge, Rick. "The Pirate Wheel." *Falkvinge.ney*. Rick Falkvinge, 13 Nov. 2011. Web. Apr. 2012. <http://falkvinge.net/pirate-wheel/>.

"International - English - The Pirate Party." *Piratpartiet.* The Swedish Pirate Party. Web. Apr. 2012. <http://www.piratpartiet.se/international/english>.

"Pirate Parties International Statutes." *Http://int.piratenpartei.de.* Pirate Parties International, 18 Apr. 2010. Web. Apr. 2012. <http://int.piratenpartei.de/wiki/images/a/a6/Statutes_of_the_Pirate_Parties_International.pdf>.

"Sonntagsfrage Bundestagswahl." *Sonntagsfrage â€" Umfragen Zur Bundestagswahl (Wahlumfrage, Wahlumfragen).* Forsa Institute, 18 Apr. 2012. Web. 21 Apr. 2012. <http://www.wahlrecht.de/umfragen/index.htm>.

"Uppsala-Deklaration." *â€" Piratenwiki.* Piraten Partei. Web. Apr. 2012. <http://wiki.piratenpartei.de/Uppsala-Deklaration>.

We Are Winning: How Pirate Parties Are Changing the World. Rick Falkvinge, Apr. 2012. Web. Apr. 2012. <http://falkvinge.net/2012/04/09/we-are-winning-how-pirate-parties-are-changing-the-world/>.

SOPA: An Objective Point of View

Evan Bull

The piracy debate has been thrust into the limelight over the past decade as online piracy has become more prevalent. With the continued growth of the Internet and pro piracy websites and groups like the Pirate Bay and pirate party promoting the spread of information and content, the issue has extended itself all the way to the United States Judiciary Committee in the form of proposed law; SOPA. SOPA or the Stop Online Piracy Act is a bill aimed at curtailing or stopping copyrighted material spread over the Internet through torrent websites. While there has been a strong opposition to the bill, there are arguments both for and against the implementation of SOPA. The aim of this paper will be to present both arguments objectively as well as attempt to measure the tangible impacts of online piracy and weigh the feasibility of SOPA. Despite the somewhat damaging effects of piracy on original content providers, the scope of the proposed SOPA legislation is too overarching and inclusive to be passed. The lack of evolution from the recording and film producing industries to adapt to an increasing digital world is an unfortunate side effect; however it is not a basis for increased Internet regulation or censorship.

In order to understand SOPA, it's important to provide a background on the history of the bill and where it currently stands. The SOPA bill was first introduced in October 2011 by Texas Republican Lamar Smith, a member of the judiciary committee. The bill stated its aims were to "promote prosperity, creativity, entrepreneurship, and innovation by combating the theft of U.S. property, and for other purposes" (Congress Library). The bill expanded the ability of US law enforcement to fight online trafficking in copyrighted intellectual property and counterfeit goods. Its main provisions included the requested court orders to bar advertising networks and payment facilities from conducting business with other infringing websites, search engines from linking to these sites, and additional court orders requiring Internet service providers to block all access to the sites (Congress Library). The law would also expand existing criminal laws to include unauthorized streaming copyright material imposing a maximum penalty of five years in prison. The implications of these provisions are massive, and will be revisited at length later in this paper. Over the course of the next several months, in large part due to a public outcry against the bill, numerous revisions and markups were made in an attempt to reach a consensus. On January 12, 2012, House sponsor Lamar Smith announced that provisions related to DNS redirection would be pulled from the bill (wired.com). In the weeks that followed, several notable file-sharing sites were taken down despite the bill not being passed into legislation. Most notably, on January 19, file sharing giant MegaUpload (which boasts 500 million users daily) was shut down by the US Department of Justice. The response to the MegaUpload shutdown was widespread. In the next 24 hours, Internet search engine Google collected over 7 million online signatures as well as coordinating an online blackout of its services in conjunction with Wikipedia (RT.com). Hacker group Anonymous launched an attack campaign the following day on Pro SOPA websites and supporters. Anonymous used LOIC or "low orbit ion cannon" software to send out temporary stress tests or TCP packets that flooded the target servers and temporarily disrupted the host. The websites of the Justice Department, FBI, Universal Music Group, the Recording Industry Association of America, the Motion Picture Association of America and Broadcast Music, Inc all reported they had been shut down (RT.com). Due to this opposition, the bill has been tabled and President Obama has stated it will not be revisited until major revisions are enacted.

Despite its nearly 80 pages in length and controversial nature, the SOPA bill itself is rather vague and leaves much to interpretation. Delving into the content it's easy to understand why the bill was drafted and its aims to expand US policy on combating piracy. One of the key problems facing the US dealing with online piracy is that many of the file sharing or torrent tracking websites are set up outside of US jurisdiction. SOPA essentially gives tools to aid the US in targeting sites within the US like search engines and social networks that may link to or advertise on foreign sites like the Pirate Bay, Zshare, or other torrent tracking and sharing sites. The bill allows US government to issue court orders and notices to US companies or actors calling them "middle men" and force the companies to stop and cut off ties or face legal action. Digging deeper into the contents of the bill there is an important section that has implications for online piracy and freedom of speech over the Internet. Section 103 line 1 states that any site or actor is dedicated to theft of US property and hereby associated as criminal if,

> The U.S. directed site is primarily designed or operated for the purpose of, has only limited purpose or use other than, or is marketed by its operator or another acting in concert with that operator for use in, offering goods or services in a manner that engages in, enables, or facilitates (Congress Library). – Section 103

Under this definition, US government will be able to shut down any site where someone posts a message, link or image that violates or infringes on copyrights or is even suspected too. Social media sites such as Facebook and YouTube are examples of business models built around the spread of information and ability for users to post content linking to sites all over the Internet. It would be very difficult for these sites to regulate everything that is posted by independent users. According to Section 103, even newspapers such as the New York Times or Economist that have comment sections could be implicated with the bill. The problem is that Section 103 allows for a "shoot first think later" mentality.

Allowing the immediate shutdown of any websites believed to be implicated or connected to illegal online piracy could have damaging effects for sites that rely heavily on user traffic and ad revenue to fund their business model. Furthermore, there are clauses in the bill that prevent any legal backlash on the US for shutting down such sites.

It's no mystery that the recording, film and publishing industries have been bleeding revenue to online piracy and file sharing for over a decade. Hollywood giants such as Universal, Sony Pictures and Warner Brothers have spent countless dollars trying to target file sharing sites and slow the inevitable decline of physical movie and music sales. The Government Accounting Office (GAO) released an extensive report stating that, "the illicit nature of counterfeiting and piracy makes estimating the economic impact of IP infringements extremely difficult" (Yager 2). Because of this relative lack of information; especially when it comes to digital piracy, we have to look to research from independent studies as well as the companies whose copyrighted material is being spread. Taking data points from each, estimates can be made for the tangible impact of digital piracy. Sanjay Jain, Professor at Texas A&M cited the Global Piracy Report in 2003 estimating 35% of software is pirated, which leads to an estimated loss of more than $31 billion to firms. The losses because of music piracy alone are estimated to be more than $10 billion (Jain 2008). Recording industry giants as well as Pro SOPA legislators have placed much loftier estimates on the yearly loss attributed to digital piracy. The US chamber of commerce has estimated $250 billion in losses a year and over 750,000 jobs lost as a result of digital piracy. While it's unsure of the exact numbers, it's likely that piracy has some tangible impact on copyrighted material.

Much of the research that supports anti SOPA arguments and points to digital piracy having little effect on the copyrighted material of the private sector ironically comes from government agencies and reputable news organizations. The research suggests the impact of digital piracy is negligible to decreasing employment or lost revenue, and in some cases may even positively contribute to corporate profits through promotional activity. In 2004, a NY Times article surfaced that questioned the validity of the $31 billion dollar loss published by the Global Piracy Report conducted by Business Software Alliance. In the article, an interview with John Gantz, the head of the research team for the BSA revealed some misleading data collection and reporting techniques.

> John Gantz, director of research for IDC, which conducted the study for the Business Software Alliance, said that perhaps one of 10 unauthorized copies might be a lost sale. In developing nations, he explained, many users cannot afford software imported from the West. Instead of describing the $31 billion number as sales lost to piracy, he said, "I would have preferred to call it the retail value of pirated software." But, Mr. Gantz said, when the trade group released the study, it termed the $31 billion as losses. (Lohr 1)

The article also interviewed Gary Shapiro, president of the Consumer Electronics Association who stated that the research seemed to assume that every unauthorized copy of a product was a lost sale. "It's a fallacious assumption that distorts the issue," Mr. Shapiro said. "And they are using this distorted data to try to get Congress to once again make copyright laws even tougher" (Lohr 1). The GAO, a government agency cited above as questioning the measurable impact of piracy also conducted research on the widely used $250 billion dollar a year loss attributed to digital pirates.

> Commonly cited estimates of U.S. industry losses due to counterfeiting have been sourced to U.S. agencies, but cannot be substantiated or traced back to an underlying data source or methodology. First, a number of industry, media, and government publications have cited an FBI estimate that U.S. businesses lose $200-$250 billion to counterfeiting on an annual basis. This estimate was contained in a 2002 FBI press release, but FBI officials told us that it has no record of source data or methodology for generating the estimate. (Yager 18)

In a more narrowly focused study on downloads of music, Harvard professors Felix Oberholzer-Gee used modeling to determine that illegal downloads have no effect on record sales. They concluded that, in contrast with industry estimates, declining sales over the period of 2000-2002 were not primarily caused by illegal downloads (Oberholzer – Gee 25). In fact, revenues generated by prominent artists were positively correlated with the number of illegal downloads suggesting the added exposure of file sharing may have attributed to increased record sales, concert attendance etc. With all of the questionable data used by Pro SOPA organizations as well as the empirical data against the negative effects of piracy, it's difficult to argue that the negative economic impact of file sharing and illegal downloading.

There is no questioning that core copyright industries have failed to evolve to an increasingly digital world. As a result, their alternative has been to launch an attack aimed at Silicon Valley and the industry leaders of technology. The online spread of information has evolved and to implement bills such as SOPA in order to regulate piracy would not only be extreme censorship, but it would be penalizing innovative companies like Google and Facebook. The unfortunate reality for the core copyright industries and the SOPA bill is that the data to support their claims is non-existent and the adaptation of the copyright industries cannot keep pace with the evolution of the Internet.

Bibliography:

"Internet Strikes Back: Anonymous' Operation Megaupload Explained â€ " RT." *RT Question More*. RT.com. Web. 01 Apr. 2012.
<http://rt.com/usa/news/anonymous-barrettbrown-sopa-megaupload-241/>.

Jain, Sanjay, "Digital Piracy: A Competitive Analysis," *Marketing Science*, July-August 2008,
27, *http://people.tamu.edu/ ~sjain/papers/published%20piracy%20paper.pdf*

Lohr, Steve. "Software Group Enters Fray Over Proposed Piracy Law." *The New York Times*. The New York Times, 19 July 2004. Web. 1 Apr. 2012. <http://www.nytimes.com/2004/07/19/technology/19piracy.html>.

Oberholzer-Gee, Felix. "File Sharing and Copyright." *Harvara Business School* (2009). Web. 1 Apr. 2012. <http://http://www.hbs.edu/research/pdf/09-132.pdf>.

"Rep. Smith Waters Down SOPA, DNS Redirects Out."*Wired.com*. Conde Nast Digital, 13 Jan. 2012. Web. 01 Apr. 2012. <http://www.wired.com/threatlevel/2012/01/dns-sopa-provision/>.

"WebCite Query Result." *Library oj Congress*. Webcite. Web. 01 Apr. 2012. <http://www.webcitation.org/643NehNoc>.

Yager, Loren. "U.S. GAO - Intellectual Property: Observations on Efforts to Quantify the Economic Effects of Counterfeit and Pirated Goods." *U.S. Government Accountability Office (U.S. GAO)*. Office of Public Affairs, 12 Apr. 2010. Web. 01 Apr. 2012. <http://www.gao.gov/products/GAO-10-423>.

Pirate Party Politics: *An understanding of the culture supporting the party and a contextualization of its political successes.*

Alexandra Catibayan

"In Europe, single-issue, fringe political parties are nothing new. But there's something different about Sweden's Piratpartiet (Pirate Party). While American politicians such as Howard Dean and Ron Paul have demonstrated the potential of the Inter- net in advancing their issues, for Sweden's Pirate Party, the Inter- net is the issue. It's the first political party in the world for which Internet policies constitute its entire party platform" (Keating 2008). The Pirate Party's success in winning its first seat in the European parliament in 2009, and then gaining its second seat after the ratification of the Lisbon treaty, marks a changing tide in the power dynamics represented in a young party and possibly a foreshadowing of political activity/ideology from the youth demographic which comprises a majority of the party members. The Party's greatest attribution for the momentum gained and needed to garner the political success it did in 2009 is due to the controversy and uproar in Sweden regarding prosecutors filing charges against the founders of the Pirate Bay, a popular and leading bittorrent file-sharing site of copyrighted materials. The Pirate Party was able to gain its initial support from the protest movement over the shutting down of the Pirate Bay in 2005, as a result of the harshening of copyright laws in Sweden, but did not gain the surge in members and support until the 2008 prosecutions against the Pirate Bay.

This activism and anger opposing major music corporation's ability to exert control over the promoted culture of file-sharing led to easily transferrable ideals, which Rickard Falkvinge would use as part of the ideological platform in establishing the party: "It's not theft; it's an infringement on a monopoly. If it was theft and it was property, we wouldn't need a copyright law, ordinary property laws would suffice... It's just not true that filesharing hurts art and artists. Musicians earn 114% more since the advent of Napster. What is true is that there's an obsolete middle market of managers" (Cadwalladr 2012). Ultimately, the Pirate Party was aiming to attack the copyright monopoly of the US record industry. This opposition against the "copyright monopoly" has permeated into other areas of the Pirate Party's political ideology: "our mission is to facilitate the emerging information society, Falkvinge says. We're a civil liberties group" (Keating 2008). Party members are opposed to and fearful of the notion of a monoculture, and a limited narrative which perpetuates the translation of a capitalist economic hierarchy over to political and social hierarchy: "what it boils down to is a privileged elite who've had a monopoly on dictating the narrative. And suddenly they're losing it. We're at a point where this old corporate industry think that, in order to survive, it has to dismantle freedom of speech" (Cadwalladr 2012). The culture of the internet simply doesn't support or understand an external body (such as the music industry or copyright laws) trying to establish and maintain rules dictating the allowable ways in which information is communicated and shared; internet culture and cyber-activists promote the culmination of ideals and information that is accessible and can be contributed to by all: "the Pirates want members to be in charge of their party and, eventually, citizens to command the government", much like citizens command the Internet (Economist 2011).

The recent success of the Pirate Party in establishing its legitimacy as an active political party and its proliferation trans-nationally, highlights the necessity to understanding the context for which the party both owes and drew its success: "when the verdict (of the Pirate Bay sentencing) was announced at 11.00am, we had 14,711 members, said Rick Falkvinge. We tripled in a week, becoming the third-biggest party in Sweden in terms of numbers" (Foreign 2009). The Pirate Party members and supporters are comprised of tech savvy, youth political activists and first-time voters, who have grown up with the proliferation of the internet and have become accustomed to the cultural implications perpetuated through human interactions via the internet.

> Given that Sweden has one of the world's highest rates of Internet usage, and that close to 2 million Swedes illegally download movies and music, it is perhaps not surprising that a party advocating an unregulated Internet would be popular. However, the Pirate Party has managed to shift the debate from downloading to civil liberties, and established themselves as the defenders of a free Internet - unshackled by the government or supranational (EU) regulation
> (Sullivan 2009).

The Pirate Party's ideologies promote digital transparency, and using the Internet as a platform to freely share information and culture. Its activism has its roots in the cyber activism carried out in response to the music industry's attack on free file sharing websites (i.e. Napster, LimeWire, etc.). It was through this cyber activism and response that, cyber-geek, Rick Falkvinge created the Pirate Party, as a legitimate attempt to garner some political activity via an offshoot party promoting the ideology of the underground cyber-activist community that was confined to the inter-web (Cadwalladr 2012). Falkvinge established the party in 2006, shortly gaining an impressive following of supporters, and by 2009, the Pirate Party became the largest "party in Sweden for voters under 30… The Pirates are geekdom gone mainstream" (Cadwalladr 2012). With the proliferation of the Internet within this generation, "geekdom" is not a unique or ostracizing trait, but rather a way of navigating the intricate and complex culture of information via the Internet, and those under 30 are the most knowledgeable and heaviest users of the Internet. The culture of the Internet has bled into the progressing of societal values within a generation that has grown in a world of technology, where the Internet is only becoming ever more accessible and developed into a daily means of communication rather than a technological luxury only available to a small percent of privileged bodies: ""The Pirate Party built a very effective Internet-based organization that's had a major impact on public debate in Sweden via blogs, chat forums, and Twitter…They clearly moved the main focus from file sharing to personal integrity on the Internet. That meant they could successfully attract people concerned that we are headed towards a Big Brother society" (Sullivan 2009). The accessibility of the Internet has become so mainstream, that the UK party promotes access to the Internet as a human right.

The leaders of this party not only promote the ideology of Internet culture to political activism and consideration, but they are exemplary bodies of the Internet culture itself. Rickard Falkvinge, a former Microsoft employee and overall computer entrepreneur, founded the party out of frustration in feeling that "Swedish political leaders were turning their country into a surveillance society" (Renee 2009). Falkvinge's frustrations with the increased surveillance of Internet activity were similar to many other underground cyber activist, and tech savvy computer entrepreneurs. This fear of a surveillance society would in turn filter through to the regular and young demographic of Internet users, who were not necessarily politically active, but were then prompted, to become politically active by the threat of their means of communication were becoming increasingly monitored and restricted. Falkvinge has used his fluency in the dissemination of information via the Internet to, then, use that technology to harness political power: Falkvinge describes how 'we're online 24/7', how they operate in what he calls 'the swarm' - nobody is in charge, and nobody can tell anybody else what to do - and how, essentially, they are the political embodiment of online activist culture" (Cadwalladr 2012). Essentially, what Falkvinge has established, is a political party that mimics the Internet culture, and promotes a flat structure in terms of hierarchy.

The Pirate Party's MEPs, additionally, are leaders representing the culture of this party. Christian Engstrom, the party's first elected member to Parliament, is a kopimist and formerly a software entrepreneur. Although he is in the minority demographic of the party, in that he is over 30 years of age, he represents the software entrepreneurs that built up the computer industry and internet software that now dictates a whole sub-culture. As a public supporter of the Pirate Bay during its trial, Engstrom was able to politicize his ideologies, and thus became a viable member and leader to be elected into Parliament, upon the Pirate Party winning its first seat.

Amelia Andersdotter is the youngest member to be elected to Parliament, as she was elected to the second seat gained by the Pirate Party after the ratification of the Lisbon Treaty. Amelia Andersdotter represents the majority of the members, in that she is a young, cyber activist who became inclined to get involved with the Pirate Party via friends. She, like many of the Pirate Party constituents, believes in the personal power that the internet provides and the exchange of culture and knowledge on the internet should be protected. She, like the rest of the Party and those who criticize copyright laws, feels that the regulation governing copyright laws are observed and outdated, and should be reformed to reflect a more practical policy regarding copyright laws. Her, and many others feel that the laws should be reformed so that copyright laws only has control for five years, as the greatest amount of monetary gains would only be in the five-year time span, as much material becomes somewhat irrelevant after that time period. This platform, of copyright law reform, looks to be both her and the other leaders' political agenda, and speak to the internet culture constructed around the openness to the sharing of ideas and files.

As the Pirate Party continues to be in the public eyes and politicize issues that so many of the young generation are entrenched in, it will continue to maintain support. The party has been able to "capitalize" on the accessibility and technology so many of its constituents are involved in, and gain growing support because it has so effectively been able to reach a concentrated audience. As they continue to stay the top of the competition by moving forward on the internet and being constantly evolving via the technology that is available, they will be able to maintain support as the younger generation will see the appeal of a party that is "on their level."

Works Cited

Cadwalladr, Carole. "Rick Falkvinge: The Swedish Radical Leading the Fight over Web Freedoms." *The Guardian*. Guardian News and Media, 21 Jan. 2012. Web. 07 Apr. 2012. <http://www.guardian.co.uk >.

"Daylight Piracy." *Economist* 400.8756 (2011): 62. *Academic Search Complete*. Web. 02 Apr. 2012.

Foreign, Staff. "Swedish Pirates Fire A Warning Shot Over Internet Censorship."*Times, The (United Kingdom)* (2009): 14. *Newspaper Source*. Web. 02 Apr. 2012.

Keating, Joshua. "Pirate Politics." *Foreign Policy* 164 (2008): 104. *Academic Search Complete*. Web. 03 Apr. 2012.

Sullivan, Tom. "Sweden's Pirate Party sets sail for Europe." *Christian Science Monitor* 08 June 2009: 6. *Newspaper Source*. Web. 07 Apr. 2012.

Intellectual Property and Piracy

Kieran Craigie

Intellectual property refers to the exclusive legal rights that person has to their work and/or creation such as music, art, inventions, discoveries, symbols, phrases, designs. The most common kind of intellectual property are trademarks, copyrights, patents, industrial design rights, trade secrets, and so on. Under intellectual property law the owner is granted exclusive rights to how their work is used.

The right for a person to legally protect their works is seen as a human right and is so stated in Article 27 of the United Nation Universal Declaration of Human Rights that "everyone has the right to the protection of the moral and material interests resulting from any scientific, literary or artistic production of which he is the author".

The most common form of illegally using someone else's intellectual property is copyright infringement. Copyright infringement is usually the unauthorized use of someone else's work for personal gain. Copyright law grants the owner exclusive rights that allow the owner to be credited for the work, gain royalties for the work, to sell the works rights, allow others to use or adapt the work, and who can use the work for financial gain. While copyright law is effective at protecting the creator's work it does have its limitations.

The biggest limitation in copyright law is that it can be protected in one country but not in another country. I am sure that many of you have heard about the book "The Hunger Games" or its movie adaption that just came out. The premise of the book has been getting wide spread criticism on the internet for its almost page by page similarity to a 1999 Japanese magna called "Battle Royale". Both stories are set in a dystopian authoritative future were each year a group of teenagers are forced to fight to the death on a reality TV show until there is only one survivor. The ending to both stories is also similar were the two remaining protagonists of the game try to work together to survive. If the "Hunger Games" and "Battle Royale" both came out in the same country there would be lawsuit over copyright infringement. But Japanese copyright laws do not extend to America.

The other major limitation of copyright law is in derivative work which is someone uses a previous creation with major copyrighted material and changes it slightly. One the best example of a derivative work is the "Mona Lisa with a

Moustache" by Marcel Duchamp in 1919. Which is exactly as it sounds, with it just being the "Mona Lisa" with just a pencil thin moustache added on. The definition of derivative work is hard to understand due to different precedent cases but the underlining thought is that the new work must have originality of its own and be artistic on its own merit.

One recent high profile case involved The Beastie Boys being sued by jazz flutist James Newton over the use of a C Note solo. The Beastie Boys used a small piece of one of James Newton's flute solos in their hit song "Pass the Mic". Newton claimed that the distinctive C Note solo was his intellectual property and that The Beastie Boys used it without his permission. The Beastie Boys argued that they received permission from James Newton's recording label and that they solo was remixed to the point that made it original and distinct. The court ended up finding in favor of The Beastie Boys.

Piracy has been defined as the unauthorized manufacturing and/or distribution of someone else's copyrighted work for one's own financial gain. Interestingly, the term piracy in reference to copyright infringement has been around since 1603. The Stationer's Company in London was given a Royal Charter granting them a monopoly on publishing. The publishers that violated the charter were labeled as pirates. It is only recently that Piracy has become an issue for internet copyright infringement.

Piracy has become a real problem due to the internet and modern recording technology that makes it easy for anyone to download, view, and copy documents, music, software, movies, and art. You can go into any city and easily find a street vendor that sells bootleg copies of new movies and music for cheap. The bootlegs are usually downloaded from a foreign country, usually from China or the Balkans, were they do not enforce U.S. copyright laws.

The major source of Internet copyright infringement is peer to peer file sharing. File sharing websites like Napster, Pirate Bay, Limewire, and others, provide links or access to movies, music, and software without physically having the copyrighted content. This makes file sharing intermediaries somewhat legal as they are not directly violating copyright law. Legal actions that are taken against file sharing websites are usually for secondary liability as they are seen as encouraging copyright infringement.

In some countries it is perfectly legal to download music and movies from file sharing sites. These countries are Canada, Spain, the Netherlands, and Panama. In Canada it is even legal to use copied material in an advertisement as long as it is not for financial gain.

There is a lot of criticism against big companies suing file sharing sites as many people online view information as a right and that companies are not really losing a lot of money. Most people who download free music don't feel bad about it because the artist/s and the company will still make hundreds of millions of dollars. Many in the recording industry are actually blamed for holding media back as they are not adapting to modern technology or marketing.

Intellectual Property and Piracy

A new form of marketing has begun in which artists and recording studios make their songs available for free by distributing them on the internet or by street vendors. The idea behind it is that more people will be exposed to the song or to the artist and then pay to see the artist live in concert or buy their merchandise. In Brazil there is Techno Brega were DJs remix old copyrighted songs and then distributed them free on file sharing sites. The DJ would then have a concert that can attract up to 12,000 to 15,000 people who all pay a cover charge making the song profitable and cuts down the cost on distribution.

Because of the easy access to songs over the internet, a new form of music genre has been on the rise and it is called sampling. Music sampling is when you use a recording or portion of a recording and mix it into a brand new song and it has become very popular in rap music. In fact one of the first sampled songs in America was in 1961 where someone sampled Elvis's "Blue Suede Shoes" and recorded it into a new song called "Blue Suede".

Major hits have been created by taking another artist's song and sampling it into another song. To legally sample some else's song you need to get permission from the artist and the label along with paying a royalty fee or a percentage of what the new song makes. Most of the big name artists like Jay-Z, Kanye West, and Eminem can easily afford to the sampling fee but it is much harder for new artists to do so. Because new artists don't have the resources of a label company they usually pirate a song and sample it without the original creator's authorization. This is usually no big deal until a sampled song starts making money in which case the original creator will usually sue over copyright infringement. This is due to the fact that copyright enforcement is usually the responsibility of the creator.

Recently, however there has been action taken by a man named Lawrence Lessig to register many audio recording under Creative Commons license that would allow legal sampling. Anyone would be free to sample Creative Commons recordings but any new recording that came from it would also need to become licensed under Creative Commons.

Legal cases pertaining to music sampling are Newton v. Diamond and Others which was The Beastie Boys and James Newton case. Another case was Bridgeport Music, Inc. v. Dimension Films were NWA was sued for sampling to guitar chords from Funkadelic's song "Get Off Your Ass and Jam". NWA sampled the song without getting permission from or compensating Funkadelic or Bridgeport Music, Inc. At first the court ruled in favor of NWA that they didn't violate copyright law but the decision was overturned in appellate court were they ruled that any sampled song regardless of length had to have permission from the legal owner. The judge on the case said "Get a license or do not sample. We do not see this as stifling creativity in any significant way."

Interestingly enough it is possible to be sued for copyright infringement even if your song has the same lyric in it. For example rapper Juvenile was sued by DJ Jubilee for using the phrase "Back That Ass Up" as both the name of the song and in the chorus. Juvenile was able to avoid copyright infringement charges by changing the spelling of ass to make it azz.

Kieran Craigie

Bibliography

Bridgeport Music, Inc., Westbound Records, Inc., vs. Dimension Films; Miramax Film Corp. UNITED STATES COURT OF APPEALS FOR THE SIXTH DISTRICT. 7 Sept. 2004. Print.

Mathis, Joe. "James Newton Sues Beastie Boys for Copyright Infringement Over Digital Sampling." *Jazz*. All About Jazz, 19 May 2000. Web. 26 Apr. 2012. <http://www.allaboutjazz.com/php/news.php?id=16>.

Natel, Bruno. "Somewhere: Tecnobrega in Brazil | XLR8R." *XLR8R*. XLR8R, 7 Apr. 2007. Web. 26 Apr. 2012. <http://www.xlr8r.com/features/2007/04/somewhere-tecnobrega-brazil>.

Paul, Stephanie. "What Are Derivative Works Under Copyright Law?" *What Are Derivative Works under Copyright Law?* legalzoom, Nov. 2011. Web. 26 Apr. 2012. <http://www.legalzoom.com/intellectual-property-rights/copyrights/what-are-derivative-works-under>.

"U.S. Copyright Office - Copyright Law of the United States." *U.S. Copyright Office*. Web. 26 Apr. 2012. <http://www.copyright.gov/title17/>.

From Sweden to Tunisia: The Development of the Pirate Party

Alexis DiSanza

From its inception in 2006, the Pirate Party has caused both intrigue and controversy. It appeals to younger generations while inspiring backlash from major industries like music, book, and film publishers. Though it began as a peripheral political party, it spread rapidly in a short number of years, becoming an international political party with a great deal of influence on local, national, and international levels. In this paper I will analyze how the Pirate Party began in Sweden and spread internationally, how the party's agenda reflects universalized ideals, and why the Tunisian Pirate Party is an example of the growing political movement.

The Pirate Party has its roots in a Swedish anti-copyright group called the *Piratebyrån,* or the Pirate Bureau. The goal of the Pirate Bureau was to promote file sharing and undermine anti-piracy political groups. In late 2003, The Pirate Bureau established the Pirate Bay, a bit-torrent-tracking website that enabled sharing of large data files in over 27 different languages (Olsson 2008). By 2004 the Pirate Bay started running separately from the Pirate Bureau and quickly grew in popularity, becoming one of the largest bit-torrent websites available. The Pirate Party emerged in Sweden from this political context. Adding to the copyright controversy, the Swedish government passed a law that made "the downloading of copyrighted material via the internet illegal" (Olsson 2008). This law effectively turned an entire generation of young people into criminals, as most people under the age of thirty had engaged in some form of copyright violation via downloads. This law caused backlash against copyright supporters, and boosted support for pro-piracy groups. The time was ripe for a political party to emerge and harness the pro-piracy sentiment that existed into political success. The Pirate Bay contributed to the growing political debate about piracy of copyrighted material, and the Pirate Party was launched as a direct result of this heated political discussion (Olsson 2008).

The Pirate Party was officially launched by Rick Falkvinge in January of 2006, and rapidly grew in popularity during the first year. Perhaps the most significant event that contributed to the growth of the Swedish Pirate Party was the May 31, 2006 raid on the Pirate Bay's servers (Olsson 2008). Some believe that the raid occurred because of international pressure to crackdown on piracy, particularly from the United States and major US film corporations. Swedish authorities confiscated servers and detained and interrogated three people in connection with the Pirate Bay (Olsson 2008). The raids came as a shock to people in Sweden, and the Pirate Party received around two thousand new members in two days. On May 24, 2006, one week before the raids, the Party had 2,174 members (PirateWeb n.d.). By June 7, 2006, just one week after the raid, the Party boasted 6,076 registered members (PirateWeb n.d.), and unprecedented increase in support. With this support, the party had a significant following ahead of the 2006 national elections.

In the 2006 elections, just nine months after the party was created, it received .63 percent of the overall vote in the Swedish national elections. Though the threshold to gain seats in the Parliament is four percent (and one percent to gain state funding) and the party was far from reaching it, it was an impressive turnout for a newly created party (Olsson 2008). This demonstrated that the Pirate Party had political appeal, and that people would switch votes from mainstream parties in order to vote for piracy issues. Another electoral success came in 2009, when the Pirate Party received 7.1 percent of the overall vote in the Swedish elections for the European Parliament, earning two seats. This victory occurred right after the Stockholm court case finished, and founders of the Pirate Bay were given jail sentences and fined after the 2006 raid (Woldt 2009). The verdict caused a new wave of support for piracy, and the party's membership tripled in a short period of time (Woldt 2009). This was a significant win because it proved that the Pirate Party could continue to garner political support for its cause. Founder Rick Falkvinge said of the 2010 election "we gained political credibility" (BBC 2011). However, this success failed to carry the Pirate Party to electoral victory in the 2010 national elections, where the party received .65 percent of the vote. This proved that the party was maintaining support, even though they clearly failed to gain the increase in votes as they had hoped. It was still the largest "small" party in Sweden by far and indicated that the party was not just a passing fad (Anderson 2010).

By the time the Pirate Party had won two seats in the European Parliament, it had already inspired the registration of piracy parties in six other European countries, marking the spread of the party internationally. The six new parties were officially registered in Austria, Germany, France, Spain, and the Czech Republic (Woldt 2009). Shortly thereafter, one of the most significant landmarks in pirate politics was the establishment of the Pirate Party International (PPI), a non-governmental organization that seeks to "facilitate cooperation between pirate parties worldwide" (BBC 2011). Surging support for piracy in Europe led to the creation of the PPI in April 2010. It is governed by a board and two co-chairs, and the General Assembly convenes at least one time per year. The organization currently has twenty six members across four continents (BBC 2011). There are also multiple countries that are not a part of the PPI that still have a registered Pirate Party, including the United States, Norway, and Argentina. In fact, there are currently sixty one states with registered pirate parties. This indicates that piracy is a worldwide ideology that has a significant amount of support regardless of international borders, particularly among young people.

The Pirate Party has experienced electoral successes in multiple countries, but it has experienced the most success in Germany. In 2009, the German Pirate Party received two percent of the vote in the national election, and in 2011 fifteen party members were elected to the State Parliament of Berlin, proving that the Pirate Party received support on both a local and national level in Germany (Essers 2012). The party has been able to maintain momentum, and in March 2012, the Pirate Party won four seats in the Saarland Parliament. Polls indicate that if a national election were held today, the Pirate Party would likely receive about six percent of the German vote, showing the progress that the party has made since its inception (BBC 2011).

Because the Pirate Party has spread internationally, the agenda that it has adopted has universal appeal across borders and is not country-specific. The Party outlines three major areas of concern for citizens at the national and international levels: to reform copyright laws, abolish patents, and improve the right to privacy (Pirate Party Declaration of Principles 3.2 2008) First, the Pirate Party aims to reform copyright laws. They believe that these laws inevitably tend to restrict information rather than promote it, which violates an underlying belief of digital piracy: that information should be accessible (Pirate Party Declaration of Principles 3.2 2008). The Party says that a copyright holder should be able to make money on their commercial work for five years after publication, because if it has not made money in that period of time, it never will. Therefore the current laws that allow copyright on commercial works for upwards of seventy five years are restrictive and unnecessary. Furthermore, the Pirate Party holds that all non-commercial works should be free from the time that they are created, and that Digital Restrictions Management (DRM) technology should be banned (Pirate Party Declaration of Principles 3.2 2008). DRM is technology used by a copyright-holding company aimed at controlling how a product is copied even if a consumer purchased it using methods like encryption and authentication systems (Noyes 2011).

The second agenda item that the Pirate Party seeks is to abolish patents. This is especially pertinent to pharmaceutical companies, and the Party holds that major pharmaceutical companies patent life-saving drugs and so they become inaccessible at a reasonable cost to consumers (particularly in the "third world"). The Party proposes that states should fund research for necessary products like drugs, which big companies carry out production and distribution of them with state oversight. In this scenario, pharmaceutical companies would still make a profit without patents (Pirate Party Declaration of Principles 3.2 2008). This is less politically controversial in Europe than it might be in the United States, as there is less stigma surrounding state involvement in private business. The Pirate Party also seeks to eliminate patents on living organisms, which they believe is unethical, as well as patents on things like software or business methods, which they believe is superfluous (Pirate Party Declaration of Principles 3.2 2008).

The final agenda item is more broad and perhaps less tangible: the right to privacy. The Pirate Party believes that the right to privacy is fundamental, and springs from other rights like the right to free speech, freedom of opinion, and the right to personal development (Pirate Party Declaration of Principles 3.2

2008). In other words, for these other basic human rights to exist, the right to privacy is paramount. The Party believes that the right to privacy must include, but is not limited to "prohibition of torture, integrity of lawmaking, due process of law, messenger immunity, and the postal secret" (Pirate Party Declaration of Principles 3.2 2008). The postal secret covers all forms of communication between individuals, including emails, phone calls, text messages, and postal mail. All three of these agenda items are universally applicable and appealing to a broad base of people across cultures, and thus contribute to the spread of the Pirate Party internationally.

Though the spread of the Pirate Party isn't new, it has most recently gained political significance in Tunisia. In early 2011, protesters managed to oust Tunisian dictator Zine El Abidine Ben Ali. The protesters utilized social media, and other technology to organize these protests in spite of government censorship, and many protest organizers had connections to the Pirate Party. Most importantly, two men, Slim Amamou and Azyz Ammami, were arrested and tortured by the Ben Ali government for disseminating information about protests (Chrisafis 2011). Amamou was later appointed as Minister of Youth and Sports in the transitional government. This was significant because it was the first time that any person associated with the Pirate Party had been appointed to a national-level political office, and it was considered to be recognition of his efforts to create an open, transparent, and democratic government (Chrisafis 2011). On May 25, 2011 Amamou resigned, stating that his mission was over because Tunisia's new democratic elections were planned (Chrisafis 2011). Still, his appointment reflected the need to recognize pirate ideology for its role in the overthrow of Ben Ali's dictatorship. Since the appointment of the new government, the Tunisian Pirate Party has been led by Sleheddine Kchok, and has gone through a lengthy battle for official recognition.

The Tunisian Pirate Party applied to be officially recognized as a political party in May 2011, but the application was rejected two months later by the Ministry of the Interior (Ghanmi 2012). The Ministry claims that the rejection was for technical reasons relating to the application, but it is far more likely that it was rejected based on the fear that the Party's insistence on transparency and openness would cause security problems for the newly organized government (Ghanmi 2012). After a lengthy appeals process, the party was granted legal recognition on March 13, 2012. There is still a great deal of discontent among youth activists in Tunisia due to the continued level of government censorship, and so it is likely that the Pirate Party could continuity to gain popularity in Tunisia, especially if elections are scheduled soon (Ghanmi 2012). Given the recent history of internet freedom and the struggle for democracy in the country, piracy is an extremely popular political ideology, and the Pirate Party could have more success in Tunisia than other places.

The Pirate Party began as a protest, and developed into a political ideology that has spread internationally. Though the Pirate Bay did not express a specific political agenda, that is exactly what sprang from its creation. The rapid spread of the party internationally is a testament to the popularity of the ideology: access to information, transparency, individual rights, and privacy. Though the party has struggled to enter mainstream politics in most countries, it has had enough electoral success to warrant serious consideration and analysis. By tracing the Pirate Party's political growth beginning in Sweden, analyzing its agenda as a set of universally applicable ideas, and through a case study of Tunisia's newly created Pirate Party, we can see that it has become a truly international ideology that appeals to people across the world.

Works Cited

Anderson, Nate. *Weeping with an eyepatch: no Pirates in Swedish parliament.* 2010. http://arstechnica.com/tech-policy/news/2010/09/weeping-with-an-eyepatch-no-pirates-in-parliament.ars (accessed April 3, 2012).

BBC. *Pirate Parties: From digital rights to political power.* October 17, 2011. http://www.bbc.com/news/technology-15288907 (accessed April 14, 2012).

Chrisafis, Angelique. *Tunisian dissident blogger quits ministerial post.* May 25, 2011. http://www.guardian.co.uk/world/2011/may/25/tunisian-dissident-blogger-minister-quits (accessed April 3, 2012).

Essers, Loek. *Pirate Party Gets Elected to Second German State Parliament.* March 26, 2012. http://www.pcworld.com/businesscenter/article/252551/pirate_party_gets_elected_to_second_german_state_parliament.html (accessed April 3, 2012).

Ghanmi, Monia. *Tunisian 'Pirate Party' gets legal approval.* March 18, 2012. http://www.magharebia.com/cocoon/awi/xhtml1/en_GB/features/awi/features/2012/03/18/feature-01 (accessed April 3, 2012).

Noyes, Katherine. *It's Time to Give Digital Rights Management the Boot.* May 4, 2011. http://www.pcworld.com/businesscenter/article/227151/its_time_to_give_digital_rights_management_the_boot.html (accessed April 3, 2012).

Olsson, Tobias and Miegel, Fredrik. "From Pirates to Politicians: The story of the Swedish file sharers who became a political party." *Democracy, Journalism And Technolgoy: New Developments in an Enlarged Europe*, 2008: 203-215.

Pirate Party Declaration of Principles 3.2. December 2008. http://docs.piratpartiet.se/Principles%203.2.pdf (accessed April 3, 2012).

PirateWeb. *Member Count History.* n.d. https://pirateweb.net/Pages/Public/Data/MemberCountHistory.aspx (accessed April 22, 2012).

Woldt, Marco. *Pro-piracy parties gain foothold across Europe.* July 23, 2009. http://edition.cnn.com/2009/SHOWBIZ/Movies/07/22/pirate.party.christian.engstrom/index.html (accessed April 3, 2012).

Cyber Warfare: The Stuxnet Virus and its Implications for Interstate Conflicts

John Emery

The 2010 Stuxnet virus attack on Iranian nuclear facilities represents a new kind of cyber-attack. Unlike the efforts to disrupt Internet access in Estonia or Georgia (blamed on Russia), or the attacks aimed at stealing American national secrets (blamed on China), this was a weapon aimed at a specific military target, which has led many to call it a "cyber-missile."[1] The Stuxnet virus is highly complex, intricate, and was designed specifically to activate with specific types of controllers that were oddly enough present in Iranian nuclear facilities. This would indicate that it was most likely not designed by individual hackers or cyber terrorists, but more likely by a team of very well funded experts, most likely sponsored by US and Israeli national governments. *Al Jazeera* reported that it is believed to have been constructed by a joint US-Israeli team as a highly efficient cyber weapon and deliberately designed to sabotage Iran's nuclear network.[2] Thus, Stuxnet has been successful at setting the nuclear program back a number of years, but not at stopping it completely. However, this "cyber missile" is indicative of the evolution of interstate warfare in 21st century conflicts, and its implications are vast. This section will explore three main questions concerning Stuxnet in contemporary warfare: What is the Stuxnet virus and how does it work? How has Stuxnet changed the way in which nations engage in acts of war? Finally, what are the implications of cyber warfare being integrated into traditional interstate warfare?

Stuxnet: What is it and how did it work against Iran?

Stuxnet was designed as a military-grade cyber weapon that specifically sought out and destroyed Iran's nuclear-fuel refining centrifuges,

---

[1] "The Meaning of Stuxnet," *Economist*, September 30, 2010. http://www.economist.com/node/ 17147862.

[2] "Iran's Nuclear Setback," Inside Story, *Al Jazeera*, January 22, 2011. http://www.aljazeera.com/programmes/insidestory/2011/01/201112273221522177.html.

possibly including the Bushehr nuclear reactor.[3] The Stuxnet 'Trojan worm' was designed "to attack industrial control systems produced by Siemen's AG", which are commonly used to manage water supplies, oil rigs, power plants and other industrial facilities.[4] The virus spreads from USB devices and exploits four zero-day vulnerabilities along with others such as the Microsoft Windows Server Service RPC Handling Remote Code Execution Vulnerability.[5] Thus, "a threat using one zero-day vulnerability by itself is a quite an event, however a threat using four zero-day vulnerabilities is extraordinary and is unique to [Stuxnet]."[6] For the Symantec internet security company, it was "the first time we have ever encountered a threat using so many unknown and unpatched vulnerabilities…which shows the extraordinary sophistication, thought, and planning that went into making Stuxnet."[7] Once the worm infects a system, it sets up communications with a remote server computer that can be used to steal data or take control of the system. In an *Al Jazeera* interview with Scott Steinberg–CEO and head of technology for the consulting firm TechSavvy Global–he stated that Stuxnet is so sophisticated because "the program is actually able to cloak itself so it gave [Iranian centrifuge] operators the impression that it was running normally, while it was actually destroying the equipment."[8] How exactly this worm specifically infiltrated the Iranian nuclear program is unknown; however, it has wiped out nearly one-fifth its centrifuges in one report and "at least 1,000" in another.[9] The spread of the virus has not been limited to Iran; nevertheless, according to Symantec–a US based computer security services company–"60 percent of the infected computers worldwide were in Iran."[10] Although Stuxnet has infected "over 60,000 computers" worldwide, its payload activated only when it found the particular system it was looking for" i.e. those present in the Iranian nuclear facilities.[11] There is little doubt that Stuxnet was initially created to directly target Iranian nuclear facilities. Ralph Langner–an

---

[3] Mark Clayton, "A year of Stuxnet: Why is the new cyberweapon's warning being ignored?," *Christian Science Monitor*, September 26, 2011, N.PAG, Academic Search Complete, EBSCOhost (accessed March 16, 2012).

[4] "Cyber Attack 'Targeted Iran,'" *Al Jazeera*, September 24, 2010, http://www.aljazeera.com /news/middleeast/2010/09/2010924201618637799.html.

[5] Liam O. Murchu, "Stuxnet Using Three Additional Zero-Day Vulnerabilities," *Symantec*, September 14, 2010, http://www.symantec.com/connect/blogs/stuxnet-using-three-additional-zero-day-vulnerabilities.

[6] Ibid.

[7] Ibid.

[8] "Iran's Nuclear Setback," January 22, 2011.

[9] Mark Clayton, "A year of Stuxnet: Why is the new cyberweapon's warning being ignored?."

[10] "Cyber Attack 'Targeted Iran,'" September 24, 2010.

[11] Mark Clayton, "A year of Stuxnet: Why is the new cyberweapon's warning being ignored?."

independent security expert in Germany who is among the first to decode Stuxnet–stated that, "code analysis makes it clear that Stuxnet is not about sending a message or proving a concept. It is about destroying its targets with the utmost military precision."[12] This endeavor was successful, and as Israeli ex-Mossad chief Meir Dagan put it, "Iran has run into technical difficulties that could delay a bomb until 2015."[13] When all the evidence is added up, from the four (unheard of) zero-day vulnerabilities, the code analysis, and the explicit design to attack the Iranian nuclear centrifuge systems, it is clear that a cyber attack of this sophistication most likely came from state actors. Thus, as an of interstate cyber warfare undertaken (presumably) by the US and Israel against Iran, it was successful to a certain degree in delaying the Iranian nuclear program, but this attack also reveals the limitations of cyber attacks in interstate conflicts.

Changing Interstate Conflict

Perhaps the greatest blessing and curse when it comes to cyber attacks is the problem of attributing from where and from whom the attack came. Countries currently enjoy the privilege of launching cyber attacks with plausible deniability. However, it is even tougher to distinguish whether it is a government or non-state actor that is committing the act. Then of course the question remains of how a nation should respond to a cyber attack against it. Should it be considered the same as any other act of war–like a bombing–to be met with a traditional military response? Or should it be met with an equally devastating cyber attack to the country suspected of the crime whether or not the government was involved in coordinating the attack? These are all very important questions that must be asked in determining what exactly states consider to be cyber warfare and most importantly how to respond to it. Moreover, it seems as though nations will be forced to erect cyber borders as the Internet has dissolved the traditional lines of nations. In the end, "attacks across borders will become state responsibilities, whether or not the state approves or guides the attack."[14] As cyber warfare becomes more integrated into traditional interstate conflict, nations will have to assume countries are behind attacks in order to be able to respond properly to attacks. Again, this becomes more complicated if one nation launches a cyber attack upon another in order to make it appear as though it was done by a different nation with both the technology and motivation in order to incite conflict that may benefit them. Nevertheless, with the increasing utilization of cyber technology into traditional warfare, states must begin to both establish greater cyber security and determine legitimate and proper responses to acts of cyber warfare undertaken by state or non-state actors

---

[12] "Iran's Nuclear Setback," January 22, 2011.

[13] Ibid.

[14] Chris C. Demchak and Peter Dombrowsky, "How Stuxnet Changed the World." *Wilson Quarterly* 35, no. 3 (Summer 2011): 57. Academic Search Complete, EBSCOhost (accessed February 8, 2012).

Cyber warfare: the stuxnet virus

Technology represents a leveling or flattening of traditional hierarchies in terms of the individual and the state, while the same holds true in future interstate conflict. The United States is currently the undisputed and unequivocal military superpower of the world. Currently the US holds approximately 5,113 active and inactive nuclear warheads, whereas China for comparison possesses about 215 total warheads.[15] Clearly the US would have the asymmetrical advantage in traditional warfare, yet China has been consistently increasing its capacity for cyber war. Recently, the congressional US-China Economic Security Review Commission (USCC) commissioned a report from Northrop Grumman, which was entitled "Occupying the Information High Ground: Chinese Capabilities for Computer Network Operations and Cyber Espionage."[16] The report obviously points out the increasing potential risk of adding cyber-warfare components to military strategy, such as China's ability to disrupt US coordination of air refueling to delay an attack.[17] However, perhaps the most important aspect of this report would be "the supply-chain risk inherent in China's increasingly dominant role as designer and manufacturer of most of the sub-components that drive modern telecommunication and computer networks."[18] Thus, China could potentially "corrupt supply chains to gain access to sensitive networks and communications, or to create the ability to control or debilitate critical systems during a time of crisis by way of vulnerabilities engineered into the integrated circuits of essential network components."[19] Essentially, China could potentially install 'kill switches' in many components utilized by US military forces that would be undetectable and would absolutely diminish the US's military superiority.

Another prominent example of how the use of cyber attacks have begun to level out the technological superiority of the US was demonstrated in December 2011 by the Iranian cyber attack that brought down the US RQ-170 spy aircraft. Iran's *FARS* news agency reported that, "the drone had been brought down through a combined effort by Iran's armed forces, air defense forces and its electronic warfare unit after the plane briefly violated the country's airspace at its eastern border."[20] Later the US confirmed that the spy plane had 'malfunctioned' and wandered into Iranian airspace, and even had the audacity to ask for Iran to return the plane to US forces. Needless to say, this did not make the Iranians happy. Ramin Mehmanparast–a spokesman for the Iranian foreign ministry–stated, "instead of an official apology for the offence they have

---

[15] "Nuclear Weapons: Who Has What at a Glance," *Arms Control Association*, 2012, http://www.armscontrol.org/factsheets/Nuclearweaponswhohaswhat#1.

[16] Benjamin A. Shobert, "China's Capacity for Cyber-War," *Asia Times*, March 15, 2012. http://www.atimes.com/atimes/China/NC15Ad01.html.

[17] Ibid.

[18] Ibid.

[19] Ibid.

[20] "Iran Military 'Downs US Drone,'" *Al Jazeera*, December 4, 2011, http://www.aljazeera. com/news/asia/2011/12/20111241599102532.html.

committed, [Obama] is raising such a demand. America must know that the violation of Iran's air space can endanger world peace and security.[21] Furthermore, in a letter to Ban Ki-moon, the UN secretary-general, Iran's ambassador to the UN said his government considered the drone incursions "tantamount to an act of hostility" and "violations and acts of aggression."[22] Nonetheless, this incident displays a few important factors for the future of cyber warfare. First and foremost, it shows how impressive military technology by a superpower is useless unless it is protected against potential cyber attacks against it. Additionally, the leveling of the playing field in interstate conflict is becoming more defined as a less powerful state can render a superpower's technology useless by simply hacking its systems. Finally, this puts pressure on the UN and the international community to determine what constitutes aggression or acts of war concerning both drone attacks and cyber attacks.

US Disadvantage in Cyber Warfare

The US is at a significant disadvantage when it comes to cyber warfare for four important reasons as outlined in Richard A. Clark and Robert K. Knake's book *Cyber War*. Primarily, the US is more dependent on cyber-controlled infrastructure than any other nation. Indeed, few adversary nations have computer networks as extensive as the US control "electric power, pipelines, airlines, railroads, distribution of consumer goods banking and contractor support of the military."[23] Secondly, most of these essential systems are not owned by the state but by private corporations. Third, these private enterprises are subject to little government regulation–most importantly being that of cyber-security systems–due to the industry's influence in the American political system through lobbying and campaign contributions. Finally and most importantly to this discussion is that the US military is vulnerable to cyber attacks as a consequence of being "netcentric."[24] Exemplified by an incident in 2009 where Iraqi insurgents used "twenty-six-dollar software to monitor the video feeds of US Predator drones through an unencrypted communications link."[25] This raises major concerns about an essential strategic element of US warfare in the Middle East through the utilization of unmanned drones for both bombing raids and reconnaissance. Although this time the technology was limited to tapping into a video feed, as Iran demonstrated, it is possible to hack the operating systems themselves and perhaps "causing the drone to return home," and bomb the US base it came from.[26] Furthermore, the US has become heavily reliant on private

---

[21] "Iran Military 'Downs US Drone,'" December 4, 2011.

[22] Ibid.

[23] Richard A. Clarke and Robert K. Knake, *Cyber War: The Next Threat to National Security and What to do About it,* (New York: HarperCollins Publishers, 2010,) 226.

[24] Ibid, 227.

[25] Ibid.

military contractors in its engagements. This is highly problematic because even if the US military were to secure its networks, the contractors often rely on public Internet that is more susceptible to being compromised. Ultimately, the US would probably be happier if cyber warfare did not exist as it represents a significant flattening of American unilateral military power and advantage.

Conclusion

The Stuxnet 'cyber-missile' represents a significant shift in interstate conflict. Based on the sophistication of the virus, it is widely believed to be undertaken by a joint US-Israeli team in order to undermine the Iranian nuclear program. Thus, the successes of Stuxnet also outline its limitations. Although it was able to delay the Iranian nuclear program by disrupting centrifuge operations for uranium enrichment, it was unable to stop it completely. As it stands, cyber warfare has become an integral part of traditional warfare and has advantages of attacking unknown sites, yet has yet to stand on its own apart from traditional methods of conflict. Ultimately, the utilization of cyber warfare by states represents a leveling of powers and traditional hierarchies of military strength. First, represented by the potential threat of supply-chain contamination by China of essential US military components. Also exemplified by the downing of the US RQ-170 Sentinel drone by the Iranians in a display of its cyber capabilities. Consequently, the US sees itself at a great disadvantage in an age of cyber conflict as it is highly vulnerable in both military and civilian aspects, while less powerful nations can render the superior US military technology ineffective through cyber attacks.

RESOURCE LIST

Books

Clarke, Richard A. and Robert K. Knake. *Cyber War: The Next Threat to National Security and   What to do About it.* New York: HarperCollins Publishers, 2010.

Journal Articles
Clayton, Mark. "A year of Stuxnet: Why is the new cyberweapon's warning being ignored?." *Christian Science Monitor.* September 26, 2011. N.PAG, Academic Search Complete, EBSCOhost (accessed March 16, 2012).
Demchak, Chris C. and Peter Dombrowsky. "How Stuxnet Changed the World." *Wilson Quarterly* 35, no. 3 (Summer 2011): 57. Academic Search Complete, EBSCOhost (accessed February 8, 2012).

Internet Sources

---

[26] Ibid.

"Cyber Attack 'Targeted Iran,'" *Al Jazeera*, September 24, 2010, http://www.aljazeera.com/news/middleeast/2010/09/2010924201618637799.html (accessed March 16, 2012).

"Iran Military 'Downs US Drone,'" *Al Jazeera*, December 4, 2011, http://www.aljazeera.com/news/asia/2011/12/20111241599102532.html. (accessed March 30, 2012).

"Iran's Nuclear Setback," Inside Story, *Al Jazeera*, January 22, 2011. http://www.aljazeera.com/programmes/insidestory/2011/01/201112273221522177.html (accessed March 16, 2012).

"The Meaning of Stuxnet" *Economist*. September 30, 2010. http://www.economist.com/node/ 17147862 (accessed March 16, 2012).

Murchu, Liam O. "Stuxnet Using Three Additional Zero-Day Vulnerabilities." *Symantec.*   September 14, 2010. http://www.symantec.com/connect/blogs/stuxnet-using-three- additional-zero-day-vulnerabilities (accessed April 20, 2012).

"Nuclear Weapons: Who Has What at a Glance." *Arms Control Association*. 2012. http://www.armscontrol.org/factsheets/Nuclearweaponswhohaswhat#1 (accessed   April 20, 2012).

Shobert, Benjamin A. "China's Capacity for Cyber-War." *Asia Times*. March 15, 2012. http://www.atimes.com/atimes/China/NC15Ad01.html (accessed April 20, 2012).

Culture Conflict

Yvonne V. Gay

There is a conflict in warfare happening now between what was and what is. I am talking about the conflict between Traditional War and Cyber War. They don't act the same but in our technology driven world these two ideas are coming in to direct conflict. The problem is that the Cyber War is different than traditional war. Cyber War and Traditional War clash for a variety of reasons from culture of the actors to tools used to carry out the war. The problem is comes from the fact that the same method of fighting a traditional wars are not affective against this new Cyber War. Can those still trying to act without taking these differences into consideration ever truly fight Cyber War? To understand and look at this question we need to take a deeper look at Cyber War.

The very origins of the act can help understand what it is today. At the beginning this was just select computer programmers manipulating code. It was a fun way to show skill and test one's ingenuity. To these computer programmers, breaking the code was a fun. They went in with the feeling that, "their work as breaking new ground by challenging old paradigms of computer science" (Douglas pg ix). This fun and exploratory nature of hacking in crucial to understanding hackers and the culture, that we find ourselves with today.

Hacking started as an exploratory art under the title of cracking because that is what they were doing to the code. Crackers were finding ways to manipulate the code to do other things in order to improve the code. There was no right or wrong implications in these activities. Morals played no part in this; it was only aimed at pushing the boundaries of the code. There was no desire to break or hinder anything just gain knowledge and experience. This distinction is where one can split these people into two generations. The older generation being crackers and the newer being what we think of today as hackers.

Crackers see themselves as separate from this new generation. They see this new generation of hackers as reckless and acting with no regard to anything or anyone. This can be seen in the reasoning that Douglas gives for the older generation using the term cracker, "hackers prefer to call their progeny "crackers" in order to differentiate themselves from what they perceive as their younger criminal counterparts." (Douglas pg ix) The beginning of *Hacker Culture* highlights this rift and shows very interesting conflict can be. This being because the newer generation does not have the same feelings of contempt at the older generation. The Hackers see themselves as doing the same thing as the older generation but better. They believe they are exploring and cracking better than ever before. They imagine themselves the epitome of what it means to crack code even though the older generation would not agree; they see these acts as pranks with a lot of the time negative consequences. Another interesting aspect of this is that many beliefs on what a hacker is and it is argued "in house". Crackers are an easily definable group but hackers are not, "to some, it is about exploration, learning, and fascination with the inner workings of the technology that surrounds us; to others, it is more about playing childish pranks." (Douglas pg. x).This is a sign that even as society wants to see this culture as unified and singular in reality internally it is not.

This generational shift did not happen out of nowhere. There are clear realities that have lead to this new generation seeing to computer world different and relating to it differently. One of the simplest differences is the age of crackers and hackers. Crackers were older and more traditionally educated. The crackers were college educated even graduate students. Their education level made them much older than the Hackers who can start hacking as a teen or earlier if they have the ability. The age of the hackers matters because of the maturity level of those involved. With hackers it is now a younger more juvenile act than the serious thing that crackers were doing.

This change could only come to be the case because of the new anonymous and autonomous, ubiquitous nature of the internet. At the time that the older generation's access to the technology was limited, "Where hackers of the 1950s, 1960s, and 1970s had little or no access to computers outside of a university environment, hackers in the 1980s and 1990s had access to the personal computer, which brought the technology that enabled hacking into their homes and schools." Douglas (pg. x) One had to be specially given the technology and allowed to use it. They were educated about how to treat and interact with the computer technology. They were a lot of the time creating the next step in the technology. They had a vested interest in the technology and maintaining a respect for their creations.

The new generation did not have those kinds of hang-ups about the technology. Douglas points out that, "these younger hackers had no institutional affiliation and no limitations on access (at least to their own machines)." (Douglas pg. xi). They had just grown up with the technology already being there. It was their playground, like a giant game to them. I have to think of it as Hackers and Crackers playing two different games. The crackers are playing chess, a complicated game where each piece plays by special rules. Essentially they are playing a game of finesse. However, hackers are pay battleship. Just picking a location and trying to sink other people's ships and cause a reaction. These games being like games of battleship, which involves lot of smack talking and immature tomfoolery. It is a fun game with little strategy or rules. This added with anonymity creates a climate for acting without restraint for a laugh, or as the internet would call it, for the LULZ. For this new generation one can act on the internet without anyone knowing who you are because the internet, "allowed for a new kind of anonymity, one that could be exploited and used to a hacker's advantage." (Douglas pg. xii).   One can say and do what they want. This anonymity can take away the feeling that internet acts need to be reflected on in real life. So if you give all this to immature people it ends with a lack of understanding for personal responsibility. This particular is something that cracker do not like about hacker culture.

Hacking culture did not stop developing here. Things could not stay so disconnected forever. Eventfully the real world started to become intertwined with the net. This could be called the LULZ with judgment. The LULZ it still very much there. Hackers still want to laugh but they also want to take up causes. Douglas points out that computers, "affords a particular avenue of resistance that speaks to broader questions." (Douglas pg. xvii) Things start to matter enough for hackers to want to act and the technology allows them the ability to reach the masses. They want to apply morals to the things that are done on the net. They want more from the net morals, causes and, even revenge. From this environment groups like Anonymous can develop and act both on the net and in the real world.

Now that we understand the culture of those engaging in hacking we need to take a good look at the differences that exist. I think to best understand this one must look at things that Traditional War takes for Granted. One of these thins is the knowledge of who the parties involved are. This is a complicated problem in itself, for many reasons. One is the fact that that there is not the guarantee that the group is to blame. One single non stat actor can be behind a Cyber War incident. Added to this the fact that one may just know an internet handle and not the real identity. It makes it very difficult to really know who the enemy is. For centuries we have been able to define both sides in a conflict and act accordingly but now we can not do that.

Tangible war is too expensive for one person to do alone. Traditional War takes a lot of money. Those engaging in it need to be able to afford man power. Lots of people are necessary and those people will need to be paid. Then there is the issue of arms. Arms are very expensive and they are necessary for Traditional War. No matter if it is knives, guns or bomb they need to be paid for. Even if one is making the arms the parts have to be acquired. The last that will take a lot of money is the actual activities. There is transportation and infrastructure that will need to be take care of as well. When all this is added up it is too much for the wealth of one person. However, in Cyber War all one really needs is a computer and internet access. Neither of those things has to be theirs. Cyber War can be engaged in from a place that provides free access to computers. The monetary limitation does not exist.

Another factor is the support of the people. Traditional War requires a certain amount of support from the people. There is the fact that a person needs people to help them fight the war. The more important fact is that they need people to not stop them from going to war. If a certain amount of the people don't support you they can band together and stop you. This is not at all true for Cyber War. With Cyber War since there can be one stand alone actor, that actor does not have to get the support of anyone else before he or she acts. There also does not need to be trust between you and the other you are working with.

Because the ties that are shared are so close that even if some band together they are still separate enough to have some anonymity and safety.

One of the biggest problems with someone trying to take Traditional War methods and use them to fight Cyber War is the expectation of a structure. In Traditional War, if one wants to cripple a movement they can take out the leader or those high up in the chain of command. The same hierarchy does not exist for Cyber War. There is no need to set up this kind of structure. At least not to that rigid an extent. Claims can be made that one is a higher up member but if really means nothing. There is no way to know if that person was in reality important, and even if that person was, someone else could quickly fill the vacuum left by that person. When there are not strong bonds there is not real reason for this one or few heads to be of ultimate importance. The free hackers still want to do what they want and there is nothing stopping them from going after that goal.

There is an inability to adapt happening here that if it does not happen Cyber War can never be combated ineffectively. The world has changed and methods of fighting have not quite caught up. It is a fundamental flaw in thought. The very definition of war needs to be rethought. Instead of thinking of it as a noun as defined: "A conflict carried on by <u>force</u> of arms, as between nations or between parties within a nation; warfare, as by land, sea, or air. -dictionary.com- Merriam-Webster" We need to think of it as an adjective for example: "Active hostility or contention; conflict; contest: a war of words.-dictionary.com A state of hostility, conflict, or antagonism A struggle or competition between opposing forces or for a particular end -Merriam-Webster" This new form of war is here to stay. So unless mindsets are changed the hackers will always win.

Work Cited

Thomas, Douglas. *Hacker culture*. Minneapolis, MN: University Of Minnesota Press, 2003. eBook.

Wikileaks and Free Speech

Nicholas Halliburton

On April 5th, 2010 a small freedom of information advocacy organization by the name of Wikileaks released a classified video taken from the gunsights of a United States Army Apache attack helicopter, showing the killing several individuals Baghdad, including two war correspondents for Reuters. The video became a viral hit, and propelled Wikileaks into the international spotlight. Two months later, on July 25th 2010, Wikileaks published, in conjunction with the news organizations *The Guardian*, *The New York Times*, and *Der Spiegel*, a comprehensive collection of over 75,000 internal U.S. military logs of the War in Afghanistan. Continuing its relationship with the newspapers, Wikileaks release the initial wave of its over 250,000 U.S. diplomatic cables in November of 2010. The public reaction to Wikileaks in the United States has been highly charged; some praised the organization as a defender of freedom of information – others accused the organization of treason and called for the assassination of its leader and public face, Julian Assange. The United States Government called for the organization to refrain from publishing the documents, citing national security concerns. It has also relentlessly attempted to cut off international funding for the organization and rumors have circulated that legal sanctions are in the works. This conflict between Wikileaks and the United States Government provides an excellent case study for the limits of free speech and freedom of the press in the United States. But in order to understand Wikileaks' situation, it is important to first have an understanding of the historical legal framework surrounding the limits of free speech in the United States.

Freedom of speech is not an absolute right; the government has the authority to limit speech in certain situations. Traditionally, the major limits surround the issues of incitement, defamation, obscenity, child pornography, commercial speech, political speech involving money, and matters of national security. This list is not comprehensive, and does not include historical limits that have since been overturned or severely limited. Some non-included examples include fighting words, prohibitions on speech related to communist political theory, or so-called 'seditious speech.' The bans on the latter two categories have been explicated invalidated by subsequent Supreme Court decisions since they were initially upheld in the 19th and early 20th centuries. The fighting words doctrine, while technically still alive, has been repeated limited in the past several decades to the point of almost universal unenforceability and no longer represents a true limit on free speech.

The first traditional limit on free speech is a prohibition on incitement to break the law. The specific threshold is represented by the 'imminent lawless action' standard established by the 1969 case *Brandenburg v. Ohio*. This case overwrote the "clear and present" danger standard that had been in place since the 1919 case *Schenck v. United States*, which is the origin of the recognizable phrase "shouting fire in a crowded theater." The new standard applied in *Brandenburg* scaled back the limit to only bar speech in which the speaker intends to incite a violation of the law that is both imminent and likely. The mere advocacy of violence or law breaking is not sufficient. A good illustration of this would be speech at Ku Klux Klan rally. If the speech took place on Klan property away from others, it would not be illegal; even if they burned crosses and called for nonspecific violence against African Americans. However, speech organizing a specific cross burning on an African American's lawn would not be protected, because it is imminently advocating breaking intimidation laws and it is highly likely that speech will be acted upon.

The next limit is defamation, which is the false or unjustified injury of the good reputation of another. Defamation in spoken form is called slander, and in written or printed form it is called libel. Unlike the other limits on speech, defamation is not a criminal matter. It is handled with tort law at a state level. However the U.S. defamation law is much different than other countries'. In *New York Times Co. v Sullivan*, the Court ruled that all statements, true or false, said about public officials are protected unless they are made with actual malice; "with knowledge that they are false or in reckless disregard of their truth or falsity." However this is an impossibly high standard to satisfy, so it has resulted in almost the total inability for any public figure to sue for defamation in the United States.

The next limit is obscenity. Obscenity is inherently not protected by the First Amendment, the government does not need to prove it has a "compelling interest" in order to regulate or ban it. However, to be qualified as obscenity the work in question must it must satisfy all three prongs of the "Miller test" established by *Miller v. California*. The first prong is that "the work, taken as a whole, appeals to the prurient interest." The second prong is "the work depicts or describes, in a patently offensive way, sexual conduct…" The final prong is that "the work, taken as a whole, lacks serious literary, artistic, political, or scientific value." While the first two are community based and can be satisfied somewhat easily, the third prong is much harder to fulfill. This has resulted in almost all forms of pornography being legal in the United States; however the government does have the authority to regulate it, such as prevent its purchase by minors. The obvious exception to this is child pornography. In *New York v. Ferber*, the court ruled that the governmental interest in protecting children from abuse outweighs any possible First Amendment protections. Child pornography is the only categorical ban on free speech; it is not subject to any qualifiers or limitations.

The next limit is on commercial speech, or speech that proposes a commercial transaction. Because the speech is inherently commercial in nature, the Commerce Clause of the United States Constitution grants the government the authority to regulate it. Unlike other limitations on speech, regulations on commercial speech usually take the form of mandates, not prohibitions. The government can force organizations to tell the truth or warn consumers about risks involved with their product. Examples of this include warnings on cigarettes, nutrition facts on food, and prohibitions on false advertising.

The next form of speech that can be limited is political speech that involves money. *Buckley v. Valeo* established that spending money to influence elections is a form of free speech. However it also established there is a legitimate governmental interest in safeguarding the integrity of the electoral process, so the government can place limits on and regulate that speech. The specific lengths that the government can go to limit this form of speech have been a subject of much focus in the last two decades, with cases such as *McConnell v. Federal Election Commission* in 2003 and *Citizens United v. Federal Election Commission* in 2010. This limit, along with the following limit, have been the two most politically debated limits on free speech in recent years.

The final traditional limit on free speech, and the one that is highly relevant to Wikileaks is speech that involves matters of national security. The government obviously has a legitimate interest in protecting the country, but the degree to which it can limit free speech and the methods it can use have been hotly debated. There are two primary ways that the government can limit free speech to protect national security; one takes place before the speech is actually made public while the other takes place after.

The first method is using prior restraint. This is when the government prevents the publication of sensitive issues, usually through court injunctions barring publication. However, the Courts have restricted and narrowed the situations in which prior restraint can be used. *Near v. Minnesota*, although it was not related to national security, established the precedent that prior restraints are almost always unconstitutional and that the government would only be allowed to use them in very select circumstances. Those circumstances were fleshed out in the landmark case, *New York Times Co. v. United States.*

In 1971 RAND employee and Pentagon military analyst Daniel Ellsberg leaked a highly classified government report on the history of the Vietnam War to the New York Times and the Washington Post. This report would become popularly known as the 'Pentagon Papers.' The papers were a detailed account of U.S. policy and military decisions surrounding the Vietnam War. The papers revealed, among other things, that the Johnson administration had systematically lied to the American public about the degree of U.S. involvement in the war and had vastly overstated the progress being made. When the New York Times attempted to publish a series of articles based on information gained from the papers, the Nixon administration obtained an injunction barring publication, citing that the information was a threat to national security. The case rose rapidly to the Supreme Court, and seventeen days from the initial publication, the Court struck down the injunctions. The Court's ruling was a fractured *per curiam* decision, with all nine justices issuing their own opinions.

Despite this, the case establishes the burden of proof that the government must meet to prevent publication: it must prove that the publication would cause "direct, immediate, and irreparable damage to the nation or its people." Some examples of this would include the publication of troop movements, war plans, decryption codes, and blueprints or schematics of war assets. Six justices found that the Pentagon papers did not meet this high burden, and therefore could not be enjoined from publication. Three justices argued that the proceedings that been unduly rushed, and it was premature for the Supreme Court to rule on this case. No justices argued that the government had met the burden of proof required to maintain the injunctions against the *Times* and the *Post*. However, five justices either hint at or explicitly say that just because the government could not bar publication of the newspapers, it did not rule out the possibility for a successful criminal conviction under statute law.

But before I move onto the relevant statute law, there is one more aspect about injunctions that are very relevant to Wikileaks and the digital age. Injunctions are not part of common law and instead fall under equity law. One of the requirements is that they must adhere to certain 'equitable considerations' or 'equitable principles.' One of these principles is that equity law remedies cannot unfairly target one party specifically over others, which translates into counts being unable to issue 'useless' injunctions. Courts can only prevent publication on information that is not already public. If the information is already available, then selectively enjoining one entity is a violation of the equitable principle. A perfect example of this principle as it relates to national defense is the Federal district court case *United States v. Progressive, Inc.* In 1979 the magazine *The Progressive* attempted to publish an in depth article that revealed the "secret of the hydrogen bomb" – the Teller-Ulam Design. The government was granted an injunction barring publication, with the district court judge ruling that in this case the government had met the high burden of proof required by *New York Times Co. v. United States*. The Progressive appealed, but before the case could be heard the Teller-Ulam Design was leaked to the public. With the information now in the public sphere and faced with the reality that the court would surely strike down the now useless injunction, the government dropped its case and withdrew its injunction. This is incredibly important to the digital age because of how easy it is to distribute and make public vast amounts of information. The result of this is that injunctions are basically no longer an available option for the government to protect national security, leaving them with only one way to do so.

That method is through criminal sanctions. The single most important piece of statute law relating to this is the Espionage Act of 1917, codified as 18 United States Code sections 792 through 799. The most relevant sections are 793 and 794. Section 793 deals with gathering, copying, transmitting, or losing defense information, and is punishable with a fine or up to ten years imprisonment. Section 794 deals with communicating defense information "to the advantage of a foreign nation" and warrants additional inspection. Subsection A prohibits communication, delivery, or transmittal of information related to the national defense, and is punishable by life imprisonment. Additionally, the death penalty can be sought if the information is found to relate to "major elements of defense strategy" such as troop movements, war plans, nuclear secrets, etcetera. Subsection B prohibits everything found in A, but also explicitly adds "collecting, recording, or publishing" to the list of prohibited actions. Violations are punishable by execution or life imprisonment. However, subsection B is only applicable during wartime.

This is somewhat relevant because although it is unlikely to be used, subsection B could in theory be applied despite the United States not officially declaring war since World War II. This is because of the *Authorization for Use of Military Force Against Terrorists*, passed on September 14, 2001. The resolution contains a provision satisfying the declaration of war requirement of the War Powers Resolution. Since it is virtually impossible to imagine the United States 'winning' this war against terrorists, as a matter of statute law, we will be in a state of war for the foreseeable future. (However the WPR has never been constitutionally vetted, so it could be invalidated by the courts.)

A common argument heard regarding Wikileaks and Julian Assange is that they are immune to U.S. prosecution because they are not United States Citizens and do not live in the United States. It turns out, this is not correct. The relevant court case here is *United States v. Alfred Zehe*. Zehe was an East German physicist that occasionally consulted for the German government in exchange for permission to travel to scientific conferences. The FBI was attempting to lure spies out from Embassy Row in Washington D.C., and was looking for a buyer of outdated sonar detection schematics for U.S. submarines. The plans were purchased by the East Germans, but they lacked the expertise to analyze the schematics. They brought the schematics to Zehe, who was in Mexico at the time. Zehe analyzed them and brought them back to East Germany. The following year while attending a scientific conference in Boston, Zehe was arrested in a public spectacle and charged under sections 793(b), 794(a), 794(c) of the Espionage Act. These sections involve copying and communicating defense secrets, as well as conspiracy. The court ruled that despite the fact that Zehe was not a U.S. citizen and his crimes took place in Mexico and Germany, he was still liable under the Espionage Act. This is because "the Act may be applied extraterritorially to both citizens and noncitizens because of the threat to national security that espionage poses." Zehe pled guilty and was handed over to East Germany in a prisoner exchange a few months later, so his case was never appealed.

So how does all of this information apply to the recent actions of Wikileaks and their leader Julian Assange? The newspapers involved face practically zero risk. *NYT v. US* sets a very high burden on the government for preventing publication. The mere *possibility* of harm is not sufficient; the government must prove that publication would cause "direct, immediate, and irreparable damage to the nation or its people." In addition, any injunction would be pointless in the digital age. Even if the government were to successfully enjoin the *New York Times*, as soon as the information was made public on the internet or by foreign newspapers such as *The Guardian* or *Der Spiegel*, the *Times* could have the injunction lifted. And although the Espionage Act does allow for the prosecution of publication during wartime, it is extremely unlikely that would ever happen. The United States has never criminally prosecuted a newspaper for publishing information. Although legally possible, doing so would most likely be politically impossible. The Obama administration has made no legal attempts to silence or prosecute the *Times* or any other newspaper.

However, the United States has used the Espionage Act countless times to prosecute whistleblowers, spies, and individuals who leak information to the press; this case is no exception. In addition to his charges under the U.S. Code of Military Justice, Bradley Manning was charged with violating section 793(e) of the Espionage Act; transmitting defense information to those not authorized to receive it, which carries a ten year maximum sentence. It is very likely that Manning will be found guilty and will face upwards of several decades in prison. His lawyers have suggested that they will attempt to mitigate his actions with an emotional distress defense, but will not challenge the facts of the case.

Finally, Wikileaks itself. Like the newspapers involved in this case, Wikileaks cannot be prevented from publishing the information they have obtained. Firstly, none of the information they have made public so far would meet the high standard required. Next, Wikileaks was prepared to invalidate any attempt by the United States to silence the organization. Using BitTorrent or other internet protocols, Wikileaks could distribute hundreds of thousands of documents in a matter of minutes. In fact, Wikileaks even went a step further than this in the buildup to the release of the Department of State diplomatic cables and the Afghanistan documents. The organization was very concerned how the United States government would respond to the leaks, so it freely distributed highly encrypted copies of all of the documents in its possession. Wikileaks then publically stated that if the U.S. government were to attempt to shut the organization down (through either legal or illegal means) it would immediately release the decryption key, granting anyone who had downloaded the files full access to all of the documents. This would ensure that there was no possible way to for the United States to prevent the information from becoming public. However, the status of criminal sanctions against Wikileaks or Julian Assange is much more ambiguous. Legally, Assange could be prosecuted under the Espionage Act. Rumors have been circulating that the Obama administration is attempting to extradite Assange to the United States so it can charge him. However, a conviction under the act is far from guaranteed. But charges against Assange, regardless of a conviction, raise several very important questions.

For example, what kind of organization is Wikileaks? It does not neatly fit on the traditional source/publisher paradigm, and in a way acts as both. This raises further questions. If Wikileaks can be charged under the Espionage Act, does that open the door for the prosecution of newspapers that publish sensitive information? Is there enough of a distinction between the two types of organizations to prevent the application of the Act? This would be an unprecedented step against freedom of the press in the United States, as the government has never prosecuted a news organization simply for publishing information.

Does Assange qualify as a journalist? Is he entitled to the special protections traditionally afforded to journalists? Many politicians, both Democrat and Republican, have stated that he is in no way a journalist. Both Vice President Joe Biden and Senate Minority Leader Mitch McConnell stated that Assange was not a journalist or whistleblower, and instead classified him as a "high-tech terrorist." And then there is the ultimate question of efficacy. Will prosecuting Wikileaks or Assange even achieve the government's goal of preventing leaks? In this situation Wikileaks' formal structure allowed the organization to distribute the leaked documents in an orderly fashion to various news outlets who could assist with the monumental task of voluntarily redacting particularly sensitive information prior to publication. If organizations like Wikileaks are shut down, will it simply force leaks 'underground' where the information will not have these additional filters? Could it even result in more harmful information being released? All of these are extremely serious questions that must be carefully considered as we look towards the future of free speech in the United States.

Works Cited

Brandenburg v. Ohio. Supreme Court. 9 June 1969. *Oyez Project*. Chicago-Kent College of Law. Web. <http://www.oyez.org/cases/1960-1969/1968/1968_492>.

Buckley v. Valeo. Supreme Court. 30 Jan. 1976. *Oyez Project*. Chicago-Kent College of Law. Web. <http://www.oyez.org/cases/1970-1979/1975/1975_75_436>.

Carter, Stephen L. "The Espionage Case Against Assange." *The Daily Beast*. Newsweek/Daily Beast, 01 Dec. 2010. Web. <http://www.thedailybeast.com/articles/2010/12/01/julian-assange-should-espionage-act-be-used-against-him.html>.

"Commercial Speech." *IT Law Wiki*. Web. <http://itlaw.wikia.com/wiki/Commercial_speech>.

"The Doctrine of Prior Restraint." *FindLaw Supreme Court Center*. Web. <http://supreme.lp.findlaw.com/constitution/amendment01/09.html>.

Dozeman, Aaron T. "The Injunction Juncture: Equitable Principles." *Partridge IP Law*. 5 Aug. 2011. Web. <http://partridgeiplaw.com/injunction-juncture-equitable-principles-meet-exclusivity-intellectual-property>.

Edgar, Harold, and Benno C. Schmidt. "The Espionage Statutes and Publication of Defense Information." *Columbia Law Review* 73.5 (1973): 929-1087. *JSTOR.org*. Andrew W. Mellon Foundation. Web. <http://www.jstor.org/stable/1121711>.

Espionage Act of 1917, 18 United States Code §§ 37-792-799. Print.

Gorin v. United States. Supreme Court. 13 Jan. 1941. *FindLaw*. Web. <http://caselaw.lp.findlaw.com/cgi-bin/getcase.pl?court=us&vol=312&invol=19>.

"Government as Regulator of the Electoral Process: Elections." *FindLaw Supreme Court Center*. Web. <http://supreme.lp.findlaw.com/constitution/amendment01/15.html>.

"Government Restraint of Content of Expression." *FindLaw Supreme Court Center*. Web.

<http://supreme.lp.findlaw.com/constitution/amendment01/18.html>
.

"Governmental Regulation of Communications Industries." *FindLaw Supreme Court Center*. Web.
<http://supreme.lp.findlaw.com/constitution/amendment01/17.html>
.

Hilliard, Francis. *The Law of Injunctions*. Philadelphia: Kay and Brother, 1869. *Google Books*. Google Inc. Web.
<http://books.google.com/books?id=PAo-AAAAIAAJ&pg=PR1#v=onepage&q&f=false>.

Jones, Ashby. "Why WikiLeaks' Assange Might Elude U.S. Prosecution." *WSJ Law Blog*. The Wall Street Journal, 30 Nov. 2010. Web.
<http://blogs.wsj.com/law/2010/11/30/why-wikileaks-assange-might-elude-us-prosecution/>.

"Maintenance of National Security and the First Amendment." *FindLaw Supreme Court Center*. Web.
<http://supreme.lp.findlaw.com/constitution/amendment01/13.html>
.

McCullagh, Declan. "WikiLeaks Could Be Vulnerable to Espionage Act." *CNET News*. CBS Interactive, 13 Dec. 2010. Web.
<http://news.cnet.com/8301-31921_3-20025430-281.html>.

Miller v. California. Supreme Court. 21 June 1973. *Oyez Project*. Chicago-Kent College of Law. Web. <http://www.oyez.org/cases/1970-1979/1971/1971_70_73>.

Near v. Minnesota. Supreme Court. 1 June 1931. *Legal Information Institute*. Cornell University Law School. Web.
<http://www.law.cornell.edu/supct/html/historics/USSC_CR_0283_0697_ZS.html>.

New York Times Co. v. Sullivan. Supreme Court. 9 Mar. 1964. *Legal Information Institute*. Cornell University Law School. Web.
<http://www.law.cornell.edu/supct/html/historics/USSC_CR_0376_0254_ZO.html>.

New York Times Co. v. United States. Supreme Court. 30 June 1971. *Oyez Project*. Chicago-Kent College of Law. Web.
<http://www.oyez.org/cases/1970-1979/1970/1970_1873>.

New York v. Ferber. Supreme Court. 2 July 1982. *Oyez Project*. Chicago-Kent College of Law. Web. <http://www.oyez.org/cases/1980-1989/1981/1981_81_55>.

S. Res. Authorization for Use of Military Force, 107th Cong., Public Law 107-40 (2001) (enacted). Print.

Schenck v. United States. Supreme Court. 3 Mar. 1919. *Oyez Project*. Chicago-Kent College of Law. Web. <http://www.oyez.org/cases/1901-1939/1918/1918_437>.

Silvergate, Harvey A. "The Real Bob Mueller." *Boston Phoenix*. Phoenix Media/Communications Group, 12 July 2001. Web.
<http://www.bostonphoenix.com/boston/news_features/this_just_in/documents/01710021.htm>.

"Subsequent Punishment: Clear and Present Danger and Other Tests." *FindLaw Supreme Court Center*. Web.
<http://supreme.lp.findlaw.com/constitution/amendment01/10.html>
.

United States v. Alfred Zehe. United States District Court, D. Massachusetts. 29 Jan. 1985. *Google Scholar*. Google Inc. Web.
<http://scholar.google.com/scholar_case?case=2028539277646161769>.

United States v. Dedeyan. Supreme Court. 19 Sept. 1978. *Leagle.com*. Leagle, Inc. Web.
<http://www.leagle.com/xmlResult.aspx?page=1&xmldoc=197862058 4F2d36_1612.xml&docbase=CSLWAR1-1950-1985&SizeDisp=7>.

United States v. Progressive, Inc. United States District Court, Western District Of Wisconsin. 28 Mar. 1979. *Bc.edu*. Boston College. Web.
<http://www.bc.edu/bc_org/avp/cas/comm/free_speech/progressive .html>.

War Powers Resolution, 50 United States Code §§ 33-1541-1548 (1973). Print.

Free Speech

Hannah Hawkings

Freedom of Speech, as defined by Merriam-Webster (2012) states: "The right to express fact and opinions subject only to reasonable limitations (as the power of the government to protect itself from a clear and present danger) guaranteed by the 1st and the 14th amendments to the U.S. Constitution and similar provisions of some state constitutions." My group focused on free speech pertaining to the Internet. I specifically focused on cases in which citizen's rights to free speech were potentially in danger. The infringement on citizen's right occurred through the removal of content on internet sites, due to reasons of indecency; patrolling of internet sites with intent to remove content, due to the intent to protect children; and by blocking content on publicly used computers, such as those in schools and libraries. Though the intentions to restrict content on those sites are well warranted and are for the safety of the young public, they are unconstitutional and violate First Amendment rights. They restrict civil liberties of American citizens.

To clarify,

> The term 'Internet' means collectively the myriad of computer and telecommunications facilities, including equipment and operating software, which comprise the interconnected world-wide network of networks that employ the Transmission Control Protocol/ Internet Protocol, or any predecessor or successor protocols to such protocol, to communicate information of all kinds by wire or radio.

(Children's Online Privacy Protection Act of 1998)

When considering free speech it is important to note this freedom is not limited to just public speaking, but rather, it encompasses other forms of expression; such as, written word, which carries into the online world in forms of web-posts, blogs, pictures and websites. Americans have the constitutional right to express their beliefs in any one of these outlets without fear of persecution or the need to censor themselves. No one should hide their beliefs because they are afraid of government prosecution or punishment.

The first case in which the United States' government attempted to censor content on the Internet was on February 8, 1996. It began with President Bill Clinton signing the Telecommunications Bill. This Bill included the Communications Decency Act (CDA), which became a federal law when President Clinton signed. The CDA was included in the Bill because the government had the intention to conceal Internet pornography. The Act wanted to expand government regulation on the new Internet media; they felt they would be able to do this because the Federal Communication Commission (FCC) already regulated the contents of television and radio content. The Act's main objective was to censor any "indecent" and "patently offensive" material on the Internet or though online communications. If the law was violated, criminal penalties would be imposed on anyone who:

> Knowingly (A) uses an interactive computer service to send to a specific person or persons under 18 years of age, of (B) uses any interactive computer service to display in a manner available to a person under 18 years of age, any comment, request, suggestion, proposal, image, or other communication that, in context, depicts or describes, in terms patently offensive as measured by contemporary community standards, sexual or excretory activities or organs

(Communications Decency Act of 1996).

Though the intentions of the court were thought to be protective of children, the American Civil Liberties Union (ACLU) claimed they were unconstitutional. The ACLU along with other non-profits, called the Act into question, which lead to the court case *Reno v. ACLU*. The basis of the ACLU case was that they found provisions of the Act to be unconstitutional and they did not abide by the First Amendment right of free speech. The ACLU was not alone, three federal judges agreed and voted in favor of their case. In June of 1997 the case was appealed, and the high court affirmed the ruling, with a 7 to 2 vote, that the CDA provisions violated First Amendment rights to free speech. Stated in the ruling of the case, the honorable judges noted: "As the most participatory form of mass speech yet developed, the Internet deserves the highest protection from government intrusions." (Liberto 1997) The provisions were overturned, and this case regarding regulation over Internet materials was the first major Supreme Court ruling dealing with the Internet. Even today this case is being examined. Recently, the Supreme Court ruled unanimously, again, that the Communications Decency Act violates the First Amendment. The Court concluded with this statement:

> The record demonstrates that the growth of the Internet has been and continues to be phenomenal. As a matter of constitutional tradition, in the absence of evidence to the contrary, we presume that governmental regulation of the content of speech is more likely to interfere with the free exchange of ideas than to encourage it. The interest in encouraging freedom of expression in a democratic society outweighs any theoretical but unproven benefit of censorship.

(Liberto 1997)

The Supreme Court took this case and the civil liberties of Americans very seriously, they extended their ruling, giving books, magazines, films, and spoken expression to materials published on the Internet, Constitutional protection to free speech.

Following this case in 1998 was the Child Online Protection Act (COPA). The intentions of COPA were good in nature. The Act wanted to restrict any material that may be harmful to minors, which could be found on the Internet. This Act was a response from lawmakers as a follow up to the downturn of the CDA; COPA focused on a more specific standard of material to be restricted; for example, instead of obscenity, or, "material harmful to minors," the restriction was directly focused on sexual acts or nudity. COPA aimed to protect minors from dangerous communication with adults with using email, instant messaging, and chat rooms. Ultimately, this law was never enforced. It was just another attempt by lawmakers to increase regulation on things such as Internet pornography and obscenities.

Instead, the Court set up a Commission. They created the Commission to conduct a study of other alternative ways, instead of COPA, to protect children while online. It was composed of 19 members separated into teams to:

> Engage in the business of providing: Internet filtering or blocking services or software; Internet access services; labeling or rating services; Internet portal or search services; domain name registration services; making content available over the Internet. And academic experts in the field of technology.

(COPA Commission 2000)

The study wanted to identify new methods to aid in the reduction of harmful materials that could be accessed by minors on the Internet. The Commission analyzed technological tools such as, "a 'one-click-away' resource; filtering or blocking software or services; labeling or rating systems; age verification systems; the establishment of a domain name for posting of any material that is harmful to minors." (COPA Commission 2000) The Commission came back with a final report in 2000. As a result of their study, the recommendation given includes: "Aggressive efforts toward public education, consumer empowerment, increased resources for enforcement of existing laws and greater use of existing technologies." (COPA Commission 2000)

COPA was never enforced and the court ruled against it because they believed it would infringe upon adults' right to protected speech. In 2004, the Supreme Court case of *Ashcroft v. ACLU*, the decision not to proceed with COPA, was upheld. The Court declared that in the time since COPA had been created, other laws had been implemented that were less restrictive to adults, while keeping children safe on the Internet. The report by the Commission in 2000 was recommended for review if families wanted to take more safety precautions.

Another Act proposed to law is the Children's Internet Protection Act (CIPA). CIPA is meant to protect children from harmful online content, like the previous Acts. CIPA (2009) was signed in 2000 and required K-12 schools and libraries within the United States, that received, "Funding for Internet access or internal connections from the E-rate program – a program that makes certain communications technology more affordable for eligible schools and libraries," to meet certain CIPA requirements if they wished to continue receiving such benefits. The requirements include protection measures that ensure the blocking and filtering to Internet sites, which contain pictures that are obscene, contain child pornography, or Internet access that may be harmful to minors.

> Schools and libraries subject to CIPA are required to adopt and implement an Internet safety policy addressing: access by minors to inappropriate matter on the Internet; the safety and security of minors when using electronic mail, chat rooms and other forms of direct electronic communications; unauthorized access, including so-called "hacking," and other unlawful activities by minors online; unauthorized disclosure, use, and dissemination of personal information regarding minors; and measures restricting minors' access to materials harmful to them.

(Children's Internet Protection Act 2009)

If the schools and libraries are able to prove they are cooperating with the requirements of CIPA, they are able to receive their funding. However, if either of these institutions fails to comply with the requirements, they are never at risk to lose funding for telephone service.

The law is focused on preventing minors from disclosing their personal information while online. However, the ACLU and the ALA reckoned CIPA unconstitutional; unfortunately for them, The United States Supreme Court disagreed and approved CIPA. The Court reasoned, "Because public libraries' use of Internet filtering software does not violate their patrons' First Amendment rights, CIPA does not induce libraries to violate the Constitution, and is a valid exercise of Congress' spending power." Also, "CIPA does not require the tracking of Internet use by minors or adults." (Children's Internet Protection Act 2009) In 2003, the decision was, not surprisingly, appealed, and again the Supreme Court upheld their decision to make CIPA law. Conversely, they did allow a revision; they altered the law so that, "An authorized person may disable the blocking or filtering measure during use by an adult to enable access for bona fide research or other lawful purposes." (Children's Internet Protection Act 2009)

Ever since 2006, the United States Congress has been debating whether to expand CIPA to include "social networking" sites. As of now, no decision has been made. Congress declares that they want to keep students safe and help regulate their activity; they do not want to abolish student's access to social networking and chat-room sites, but rather, help to protect them.

Free speech on the Internet is an important civil liberty to protect; this is something the Electronic Frontier Foundation (EFF) agrees with. The EFF was founded in the early days of the Internet in 1990, when most people were not even acquainted with the World Wide Web. The organization was founded that July because of a threat to free speech, introduced by The United States Secret Service Agents. The incident occurred when a BellSouth computer, containing information as to how the 911 emergency systems worked, was hacked. The

Secret Service became paranoid, and, understandably, instantly assumed worst-case scenario. They feared that the "hackers" would wrongly use the information they had acquired; they, hypothetically, would do this by busying the safety lines, which would prevent those who were calling for true emergencies, to receive help. This fear led to a series of raids by the Secret Service looking to uncover the distribution source of the illegally copied document.

The Secret Service believed Steve Jackson, one of several, was in possession of the document, so he became a victim of the raid, though he was innocent. His electronic equipment was seized, examined, and, unfortunately for him, important files and emails were deleted. Due to his computers being gone, his business was destroyed because he was unable to access his files. Jackson was livid, and rightly so,

> He believed his rights as a publisher had been violated and the free speech and privacy rights of his users had been violated. Steve Jackson tried desperately to find a civil liberties group to help him, to no avail. Unfortunately, none of the existing groups understood the technology well enough to understand the importance of the issues.
> (Electronic Frontier Foundation 2012)

Luckily, Jackson found hope in Mitch Kapor, John Barlow, and John Gilmore, all informed technologists. The four came together and they, "Formed an organization to work on civil liberties issues raised by new technologies," (Electronic Frontier Foundation 2012) which would come to be known as The Electronic Frontier Foundation (EFF). The group filed a lawsuit against the Secret Service, which was known as *The Steve Jackson Games* case. This was the first cyberspace case; fortuitously, when EFF won, the groundwork had been laid for electronic mail and the protection it deserves. The Court declared, "Electronic mail deserves at least as much protection as telephone calls . . . Law enforcement must have a warrant that particularly describes all electronic mail messages before seizing and reading them." (Electronic Frontier Foundation 2012)

The organization has continued to fight for rights to free speech. When they know free speech is in jeopardy they rally to help and provide the best legal defense. A more recent example of their work is the encryption case against Dan Bernstein. EFF came together and their work paid off: "The court ruled that the export control laws on encryption violated Bernstein's First Amendment rights by prohibiting his constitutionally protected speech," (Electronic Frontier Foundation 2012) the group had done it! "The court had ruled, for the first time ever, that written software code is speech protected by the First Amendment." (Electronic Frontier Foundation 2012)

To represent and provide awareness of the threats to free speech in new media, the EFF has organized a successful campaign called the Blue Ribbon Campaign. The campaign has developed made a presence on the Internet. It was created to campaign for intellectual freedom online. Its aim is to encourage website owners to place images of blue ribbons on their own websites. If a website owner does so, it shows they are in support of free speech and intellectual freedom on the Internet.

It is very clear that there are many people and organizations, who value their right to free speech in any arena of expression; they will go to great lengths to ensure their liberties will not be taken away or restricted. This is what is great about America, when people believe in something and want something bad enough, generally, they make it happen, especially if they have the right to do so. Americans will continue to protect their rights and fight lawmakers when they fear infringement on their rights. Freedom of speech will always be a coveted civil liberty.

Works Cited

Children's Online Privacy Protection Act of 1998. 1998. *Accessed: 1 April 2012*
    <http://www.ftc.gov/ogc/coppa1.htm>.

Children's Internet Protection Act. 2009. *Federal Communications Commission. Accessed: 1 April 2012 <http://www.fcc.gov/guides/childrens-internet-protection-act>.*

Communications Decency Act of 1996. 1996. *Accessed: 20 April 2012*
    <http://www.netjaunt.com/thinkinghurts/decencyact.txt>.

COPA Commission. 2000. *The Congressional Internet Caucus Advisory Committee. Accessed: 2 April 2012 <http://www.copacommission.org/>.*

Electronic Frontier Foundation. Electronic Frontier Foundation. 2012 Accessed: 2 April 2012 <https://www.eff.org/about>.

Liberto, Shelley. 1997. "Supreme Court Strikes Down Decency Act in Defense of Internet 'Chaos'." Law Offices of Shelley M. Liberto. Accessed: 10 April 2012 <http://www.libertolaw.com/profile_a9.html >.

Merriam-Webster. 2012. Merriam-Webster, Inc. Accessed: 1 April 2012
    <http://www.merriam-webster.com/dictionary/censorship>.

Reno v. American Civil Liberties Union. 1997. *521 U.S. 844. Accessed: 1 April 2012*
    <http://law2.umkc.edu/faculty/projects/ftrials/conlaw/reno.html>.

Freedom of Speech on the Internet: The Role of the Internet in the Middle East Uprisings

Joshua Kellems

In Western Society, it is easy to take for granted the amount of freedoms that we have, especially those surrounding the internet. Individuals in the west have nearly unfiltered access to an infinite amount of information and are free to say or post whatever they like. Unfortunately, this is not the case in the Middle East where many totalitarian regimes have censored and restricted access to a great deal of information on the internet. However, with the help of the internet and popular social media sites, individuals were able to spark unprecedented revolutions that would spread across the Middle East despite the vast amount of censorship and surveillance. In order to gain a better understanding of the harsh restrictions placed on internet freedom in the Middle East, we will analyze the Internet censorship and surveillance laws of four Middle Eastern countries: Egypt, Tunisia, Iran, and Syria. And finally, we will review the Egyptian Revolution including the origins of unrest within the country as well as the integral role the internet played in its success.

Egypt

Prior to the mass protests that removed Hosni Mubarak from office; Egyptians had nearly unfiltered access to the internet as its use was heavily promoted by the government. However, there was a great deal of surveillance. All internet café managers and owners were required by law, and the Egyptian Ministry of Interior, to record the names and identification card numbers of all customers. Those that refused to comply risked being shut down and losing their business. Popular social media sites like Facebook and other blogs are under constant surveillance and those "the state deem harmful to public security are often arrested, denied access to the internet, and harassed by the state police," (opennet.net). Comments that are deemed to be harmful to state security included insults to the president, something that blogger Kareem Amer was sentenced to four years in prison for as well as "incitement to hatred of Islam." He has since become a recognized symbol of online repression to the bloggers all over the Middle East. Finally, in 2009, access to pornography on the internet was outlawed as it was deemed offensive to religion and societal values.

Freedom of Speech on the Internet:

Tunisia

Prior to the protests that saw Ben Ali ousted from power in Tunisia, the country had one of the most developed telecommunications structures in The Middle East and North Africa. However, it was extremely filtered and suppressed opposition and critical speech with many "opposition and dissident Web sites and blogs have been victims of hacking attempts and in some cases, successful content removal and shutting down of servers,"(opennet.net). Like many other countries in the region, they censor popular social media websites and at one point in 2007 actually blocked all access to Facebook.

In order to heavily filter what people can see on the internet, the Tunisian government actually uses American made technology. Using software known as SmartFilter, all websites and domains that they deem harmful to the security of the state are blocked. The software is designed to show a standard 404 "Forbidden" message, but the Tunisian government has altered it so that it reads 403 "File Not Found" message in order to mask how much information they were truly blocking access to.

Iran

Over the past decade, Iran has had the highest rate of growth for internet use, at 48% a year, than any other Middle Eastern country. It also happens to have one of the most expansive internet filtering systems in the world as well as a growing internet surveillance movement. The Revolutionary Guard has begun to play an integral role in the enforcement of internet censorship laws as well as the censorship of objectionable material online. That role has also grown to include the use of pro-state bloggers to control and locate dissident speech online. Due to the advanced surveillance system in place, the authorities are able to read emails and instant messages that could implicate citizens that speak out against the government or Islam. Many of the popular social media websites are either blocked or under heavy surveillance, while all topics related to sexuality are blocked.

All internet access points in the country must be connected to a state run telecommunications provider or risk being imprisoned. Iranian citizens are limited to what they are able to view as the Supreme Council of the Cultural Revolution (SCRC) required all Iranian internet service providers to install filtering systems. A subcommittee of the SCRC, the Committee of Determining Unauthorized Sites (CCDUS), was set up in order to "set criteria for identifying unauthorized websites to be blocked," (opennet.net). This agency also determines what domain names to block as well.

Syria

Syria has the least developed telecommunications system in the Middle East, but also the most regulated. Almost all media is controlled by the government or the ruling Baath Party making any criticism of the government or the President illegal. Interestingly enough, the Syrian constitution calls for freedom of speech and the press, however, the government has found a loophole. Since 1962, the government has had the Emergency Law enacted leaving Syria in a constant state of emergency for the last fifty years. This allows the government to heavily restrict publications, censor the internet, and imprison or harass anyone they deem harmful to the state without question. Journalists and political activists "risk arrest at any time for virtually any reason and are "up against a whimsical and vengeful state apparatus which continually adds to the list of things banned or forbidden to be mentioned,"(Wired). It has been ranked consistently by Reporters Without Borders as one of the thirteen enemies of the internet, a title they share with other countries such as Belarus, China, and North Korea.

Internet users are under constant surveillance, especially internet café users who are required to submit their names and ID numbers to the café manager. Those that do not comply lose access to the internet and the cafes that do not comply are forced with the prospect of being shut down. Because of the heavy use of surveillance and the civilians inability to fully gauge what can be construed as dissident speech; many Syrians perform self-censorship in an effort to reduce the risk of imprisonment or censorship by the government.

Now that we have a better understanding of the restrictions surrounding the internet in these specific Middle East and North African countries, let us take a look at how average citizens were able to use the internet in order to foster revolution despite extreme disadvantage.

Origins of Unrest: Egypt

There are many factors that led to the outrage that sparked revolution in Egypt, most having to do with government corruption and unaccountability. In 2008 Egypt experienced an extreme rise in inflation and grain shortages that led to the Bread Crisis of 2008. During this time, families would wait for hours standing in line to receive their family's daily bread rations. Many would not even receive their rations. Then during the swine flu outbreak, the Egyptian government went against the recommendations of the United Nations and slaughtered close to 300,000 pigs in an attempt to combat the risk of infection. There was no evidence to suggest that the disease was passed directly from pigs to humans and the owners of the pigs were poorly compensated or not compensated at all.

In Egypt, most of the waste is collected and recycled by the lower classes and is their source of income. However, the government decided to "modernize" their waste collection practices by privatizing it and granting a $50 million contract to a foreign trash collecting firm. This firm was only required to collect and recycle 20% of the material while the lower classes were able to recycle nearly 80% of it. Then, showing the extreme oppression of the state, a young man named Khaled Said was brutally beaten to death by police for trying to show police corruption on YouTube. The economy was continuing to do poorly and in a desperate act of protest, a young man sets himself on fire outside of parliament in order to bring attention to the extreme high unemployment and inflation that the government does nothing about. The next day, 18 January 2011, a young woman named Asmaa Mahfouz post a video on YouTube calling on people to join her in Tahrir Square on the 25th of January in order to peacefully protest the government. She is credited with establishing the mass protests.

Organizing the Protests

Following the post by Asmaa calling on people to join her in Tahrir Square, a Facebook page was created which gathered thousands of followers a second. When the day of protest was upon them, organizers looked to twitter to get the word out and update people as to the condition and meeting places for the actual protests. Twitter was eventually blocked, but the main activists were able to still get messages out via a proxy server. According to one protest organizer "a revolution planned on Facebook, organized on Twitter and broadcast to the world via YouTube," (Mason 14).

The initial government reaction to the protests was to deploy riot police and the military to keep the peace but violent clashes erupted among the protester, the government loyalists and the secret police. Twitter was eventually blocked in an attempt to disorganize the protests but activists were still able to get the message out via a proxy service. Finally after two days of fierce protest roughly 88% of the internet is shut down, however it is too late. The protests had grown so large that the world was taking notice. Mubarak is forced to step down.

The revolutions that occurred in Tunisia and Egypt would inspire change in the Middle East, as these two countries provided a template for other countries to follow. Facing perceived insurmountable odds in harsh surveillance states where freedom of speech on the internet was extremely limited, people were still able to react against the government and bring about change thanks to simple social media and the internet.

Sources:

http://opennet.net/research/profiles/egypt
http://opennet.net/research/profiles/tunisia
http://opennet.net/research/profiles/iran
http://opennet.net/research/profiles/syria
http://www.wired.com/dangerroom/2011/01/egypts-internet-shutdown-cant-stop-mass-protests/
http://www.guardian.co.uk/world/interactive/2011/mar/22/middle-east-protest-interactive-timeline
http://www.wired.com/dangerroom/2011/01/egypts-internet-shutdown-cant-stop-mass-protests/
http://www.hrw.org/news/2011/02/08/egypt-inspired-protests-across-middle-east-meet-violent-clampdown
Mason, Paul. *Why It's Kicking off Everywhere: The New Global Revolutions*. London: Verso, 2012. Print.

From Citizen to Suspect: Freedom of Speech and the Patriot Act

Jack Mallahan

When the United States of America suffered the deadliest terrorist attack in history on September 11, 2001, the government decided that drastic changes needed to be made to the National Security policy. As a result of these attacks, the USA PATRIOT Act (The Uniting and Strengthening America by Providing Appropriate Tools Required to Intercept and Obstruct Terrorism Act) was signed into law on October 26, just a little over a month after the attack. This comprehensive act's intent was to expand the government's ability to investigate terrorism. However, there has been much controversy surrounding the Patriot Act, especially pertaining to suppression of speech. The Patriot Act gives the government unprecedented power to investigate, track, and detain US citizens without probable cause. Although the USA PATRIOT Act was signed into law with the intent to promote national security, many parts of the act are unconstitutional and suppress freedom of speech and expression on the internet.

It is necessary to understand that context of how this monumental bill was able to pass with 357 Yeas and 66 Nays in the House and 98 Yeas and only 1 Nay in the Senate, . After the attacks on 9/11, there was a strong bipartisan push to strengthen the nation's security. This brought Republican Congressman F. James Sensenbrenner to sponsor the Patriot Act, and the bill was introduced to the House of Representatives on October 23rd and passed both the House and the Senate by the 25th. This 340-page bill is composed of ten titles: Enhancing Domestic Security against Terrorism, Surveillance procedures, Anti-money-laundering to prevent terrorism, Border security, Removing obstacles to investigating terrorism, Victims and families of victims of terrorism, Increased information sharing for critical infrastructure protection, Terrorism criminal law, Improved Intelligence, and Miscellaneous (Bill Text). The size of the bill and the speed at which it was passed have been the focal point of much controversy, with many saying that the Patriot Act was passed opportunistically with little debate or editing. In one of the scenes of Michael Moore's 2004 film "Fahrenheit 9/11," Moore records Congressman Jim McDermott alleging that no Senator read the bill and John Conyers, Jr. as saying, "We don't read most of the bills. Do you really know what that would entail if we read every bill that we passed?" Congressman Conyers then answers his own rhetorical question, asserting that if they did it would "slow down the legislative process" (Fahrenheit 9/11). Because of the speed this legislation passed through congress, many sections of the Patriot Act are unconstitutional and violate the privacy of US citizens, including many sections in Title II: Surveillance procedures.

While the intent of Title II in the USA PATRIOT Act is to increase the power of surveillance of various government agencies in an attempt to counter terrorism, Title II violates citizens' first and fourth amendment rights. Within Title II is Section 212 which expands the scope of subpoenas to Internet Service Providers (ISPs) to include "the name, address, local and long distance telephone toll billing records, telephone number or other subscriber number or identity, and length of service of a subscriber" but also session times and durations, types of services used, communication device address information (IP Addresses) payment method and bank account and credit card numbers. Communication providers are also allowed to disclose customer records or communications if they suspect there is a danger to "life and limb," or more disturbingly "if the service provider believes that they must do so to protect their rights or property" (EPIC). There is no further explanation of what circumstances warrant the release of this information. This means that ISPs can release all of this information about any subscribers to the government without a court order, clearly breaking the Fourth Amendment right "to be secure in their persons, houses, papers, and effects, against unreasonable searches and seizures" (The US Constitution). But this is not the only example within Title II where vaguely worded statutes further force people to censor themselves.

Although US citizens are guaranteed freedom of speech, religion, and association in the Constitution, Section 215 of the USA PATRIOT Act violates freedoms which are supposed to be protected under the First Amendment. Under Section 215, the FBI can investigate US citizens based at least in part on their exercise of First Amendment rights and can investigate non-U.S. persons based solely on their free speech activities or religious practices. Anyone could be investigated based on, "the political or religious meetings they attend the websites they visit or even the books that they read" (EPIC). This allows for the government to watch any US citizen, including practices such as "going undercover to infiltrate an organization, going through trash, following the person or group for extended periods of time, taking pictures, and doing extensive background checks—all without a warrant or even suspicion of criminal activity" (Civil Liberties Issues). This has led to many refraining from exercising their Constitutional rights in self-censorship out of fear; attendance at and donations to mosques have dropped significantly, as many Muslims reasonably fear that they will be targeted for investigation based solely on their religious beliefs (Patriot Act Fears). But that is not all Section 215 does, it permits the FBI to seek records from bookstores and libraries of books that a person has purchased or read, and/or his or her activities on a library's computer. This allows the government to violate individuals' First Amendment rights to, "read, recommend, or discuss a book, to write an email, or to participate in a chat room. It also denies booksellers and library personnel their free speech rights by preventing them from informing anyone, including the subject of the search, about the request for the release of information" (Civil Liberties Issues). This allows the government to track anyone because of his or her actions at public libraries, an institution created for research. This section forces US citizens to censor themselves when expressing their academic curiosity, out of fear of being watched by the FBI. This fear is well founded because of the National Security Letter provision in Title V of the Patriot Act.

The National Security Letter provision in the Patriot Act radically expanded the FBI's authority to demand personal customer records from Internet Service Providers, financial institutions and credit companies without a warrant, clearly violating the First and Fourth Amendments. Using NSLs, the FBI can collect vast amounts of information about innocent people and obtain sensitive information such as, "the web sites a person visits, a list of e-mail addresses with which a person has corresponded, or even unmask the identity of a person who has posted anonymous speech on a political website" (National Security Letters). Not only can the FBI collect extensive, private information about a person without reasonable doubt, the provision also allows the FBI to forbid or "gag" anyone who receives an NSL from telling anyone about the record demand (National Security Letters). Nicholas Merrill, founder of Calyx Internet Access and the Calyx Institute, was faced with this situation when he received a NSL in 2004. The letter requested that Merrill provide 16 categories of "electronic communication transactional records," including e-mail address, account number and billing information. Most of the other categories remain redacted by the FBI (Merrill, Nicholas). But because of the "gag" order, Merrill was not allowed to tell anyone that he had received this NSL, a clear breach of freedom of speech. In fact, Merrill's "gag" was partially lifted after 6 years, when the FBI decided they no longer wanted the information they were seeking. Although the FBI abandoned their query, many things are redacted from the record and Merrill is still unable to talk about much of the situation. But National Security Letters are not the only legal actions in place preventing freedom of speech on the internet by the Patriot Act.

At first glance, it seems as if Title VII of the Patriot Act would be the least controversial because its premise is "Strengthening the Criminal Laws Against Terrorism," but in reality this title has been used to suppress free and peaceful speech (Bill Text). Section 805 illicitly states that providing "material support" to any foreign organization the Secretary of State has designated as terrorist is deemed an act of terrorism (Bill Text). "Material support" is defined in the statute to include almost any kind of support for blacklisted groups, including "humanitarian aid, training, expert advice, 'services' in almost any form, and political advocacy" (Eagan, Timothy). This loose definition of "material support" is where freedom of speech is infringed upon. In 2004, Sami Omar al-Hussayen was arrested in Moscow, Idaho for aiding terrorists by providing, "expert guidance" to groups deemed terrorist groups. Al-Hussayen was a graduate student at the University of Idaho, where he had organized a candle-light vigil a few days after the attacks on 9/11 to pray for the victims and condemn the terrorists (Eagan, Timothy). However, this man who had helped lead peaceful demonstrations was arrested based on accusations of plotting to aid and to maintain Islamic Web sites that promote jihad. As a Web master to several Islamic organizations, al-Hussayen helped to maintain several Internet sites with links to groups that praised suicide bombings in Chechnya and in Israel.

But he himself does not hold those views. His role was like that of a technical editor, and his lawyers argued that he cannot be held criminally liable for what others wrote (Eagan, Timothy). The prosecutors claimed that al-Hussayen donated money to organizations that raise funds for violent jihad, but al-Hussayen's lawyers said that he gave money to "legitimate Islamic charities and that his Web site work was protected by the First Amendment. The Web sites he maintained also posted views opposing jihad, they said" (Eagan, Timothy). Although al-Hussayen was acquitted on all three charges of terrorism, he was still held by immigration authorities until he was deported in July 2004 (Eagan, Timothy). Al-Hussayen's arrest was based on such an indirect connection to terrorism that David Cole, a well known Georgetown University law professor (and lawyer for The Humanitarian Law Project) was so appalled by al-Hussayen's arrest that he claimed, "somebody who fixes a fax machine that is owned by a group that may advocate terrorism could be liable" (Eagan, Timothy). But it wasn't just Muslims who were affected by Section 805 of the Patriot Act.

Although The Humanitarian Law Project (HLP) is a non-profit organization that works to protect human rights and promote "the peaceful resolution of conflict by using established international human rights laws and humanitarian law," it was also attacked under Section 805 of the Patriot Act (Humanitarian Law Project). Ralph Fertig, the founder of The Humanitarian Law Project, has helped the Kurdistan Workers' Party (PKK) make human rights claims before international bodies. The HLP has trained Kurdish leaders in peacemaking negotiations and have brought them to Washington to lobby (Totenberg, Nina). But since the PKK became listed as a terrorist organization with the passing of the Patriot Act, The HLP had to cut all ties. David Cole, the lawyer representing the Humanitarian Law Project said, "The interest in stopping even pure speech, furthering no illegal ends, simply because you don't like an organization because you decided to make an organization 'radioactive,' is impermissible under our First Amendment" (Totenberg, Nina). The HLP's urging of the PKK to put down its arms and offering to assist the PKK to negotiate peaceful negotiations went all the way to the Supreme Court on June 21, 2010 (Holder v. Humanitarian Law Project). The Supreme Court decision marks the first time that the Supreme Court has held that the "First Amendment permits Congress to make pure speech advocating lawful, nonviolent activity-human rights advocacy and peacemaking-a crime. Doing so can land a citizen in prison for 15 years, all in the name of fighting terrorism" (Holder v. Humanitarian Project). So although the HLP's goal is to prevent violence, it would be a crime for them to try to help bring peace between the Kurds and the Turks. This is clearly a terrifying precedent set against the First Amendment, censoring even peaceful free-speech.

While the USA PATRIOT Act was drafted with the good intentions of protecting citizens from terrorism, the act has infringed on the constitutional rights of citizens, especially free speech. There are blatant contradictions to the First and Fourth Amendments to the Constitution in Titles II and V, but that is not all. With the speed at which the bill was written and then passed, there are many clauses and sections with vague wording allowing for the government to interpret the act in other unconstitutional ways. Senator Ron Wyden (D-Ore.), a member of the Senate Intelligence Committee even said, "When the American people find out how their government has secretly interpreted the Patriot Act, they will be stunned and they will be angry" (Merrill, Nicholas). This is more proof that the USA PATRIOT Act needs to be over-turned because of its policy of turning US citizens into suspects and the ability for the government to nullify constitutional rights.

Works Cited

"Bill Text 107th Congress (2001-2002) H.R.3162.ENR." *Bill Text*. The Library of Congress, 26 Oct. 2001. Web. 21 Apr. 2012. <http://thomas.loc.gov/cgi-bin/query/D?c107:4:./temp/~c107oTkE3b::>.

"Civil Liberties Issues." *BORDC: Freedom of Speech, Religion, and Assembly*. Bill of Rights Defense   Committee, 18 Aug. 2011. Web. 23 Apr. 2012. <http://www.bordc.org/threats/speech.php>.

The Constitution of the United States. *Senate.gov*. U.S. Senate. Web. 22 Apr. 2012. <http://www.senate.gov/civics/constitution_item/constitution.htm>.

Eagan, Timothy. "Computer Student on Trial Over Muslim Web Site Work."*Nytimes.com*. The New York Times, 27 Apr. 2004. Web. 23 Apr. 2012. <http://www.nytimes.com/2004/04/27/us/computer-student-on-trial-over-muslim-web-site- work.html?pagewanted=all>.

"EPIC - USA Patriot Act." *Epic.org*. Electronic Privacy Information Center. Web. 23 Apr. 2012. <http://epic.org/privacy/terrorism/usapatriot/>.

Fahrenheit 9/11. By Michael Moore. Dir. Michael Moore. Studio Canal, 2004. DVD.

"Holder v. Humanitarian Law Project." *Washington Post*. The Washington Post, 22 June 2010. Web.   23 Apr. 2012. <http://www.washingtonpost.com/wpdyn/content/article/2010/06/21/AR2010062104267.html>.

"Humanitarian Law Project." *Humanitarian Law Project*. Web. 23 Apr. 2012. <http://hlp.home.igc.org/>.

Merrill, Nicholas. "How the Patriot Act Stripped Me of My Free-speech Rights."*Washington Post*. The Washington Post, 26 Oct. 2011. Web. 22 Apr. 2012. <http://www.washingtonpost.com/opinions/how-the-patriot-act-stripped-me-of-my-free-speechrights/2011/10/20/gIQAXB53GM_story.html>.

"National Security Letters." *Aclu.org.* American Civil Liberties Union, 10 Jan. 2011. Web. 22 Apr. 2012. <http://www.aclu.org/national-security-technology-and-liberty/national-security-letters>.

"PATRIOT Act Fears Are Stifling Free Speech, ACLU Says in Challenge to Law."*Aclu.org.* American Civil Liberties Union, 3 Nov. 2003. Web. 22 Apr. 2012. <http://www.aclu.org/national-security/patriot-act-fears-are-stifling-free-speech-aclu-says-challenge-law>.

Totenberg, Nina. "Does The Patriot Act Violate Free Speech?" *NPR.* NPR, 23 Feb. 2010. Web. 23 Apr. 2012. <http://www.npr.org/templates/story/story.php?storyId=123993822>.

"The USA Patriot Act Highlights. *The United States Department of Justice.* Web. 22 Apr. 2012. <http://www.justice.gov/archive/ll/highlights.htm>.

Anonymous: The Social Organism

Dustin Phillips

Since the commercialization of the internet in 1995, it has grown exponentially. With the next few years, came the first web-based email, the Google revolution, and the proliferation of file-sharing among the mainstream public. This drastically changed the way in which people communicated, acquired information, and shared music. A more significant consequence of the internet's coming of age is the decentralized atmosphere that has become a part of everyday life today. People were no longer reliant on traditional forms of communication, such as the telephone and postal service. Libraries lost their monopoly on information, and Sam Goody was no longer the place to go for music. This decentralization, along with the new ease of transferring information, led to a new collaborative and open-source mentality. A new form of Silicon Valley was born.

The dissemination of information across the internet created a new array of possibilities. The internet became a forum for people to come together and collaborate on collective projects. Exemplary of projects of this kind are Wikipedia, Linux, and YouTube. However, limiting the impact to technological innovation would be a much too narrow view. The spread of ideas has been just as important as the spread of information, although it can be hard to differentiate the two at times. The spread of information has been made possible through social media, blogs, chat rooms, image boards, etc. The search for others with similar interests and beliefs often leads the seekers to these destinations. This phenomenon that exemplifies internet culture is the impetus that led to the formation of Anonymous.

What is Anonymous?

Describing what Anonymous is not is much easier task than describing what it is. It is neither a group, nor a club. There is no hierarchy, centralization, or formal membership. It has been describe as a collective, an idea, a meme, and as a culture. However, to properly address an unprecedented movement, it is sometimes necessary to describe it in more abstract terms. One term that seems to portray Anonymous well, is the term "social organism." A social organism is a society or societal structure that is viewed as a living organism. Anonymous fits this description, because it reacts with its surroundings fluidly, adapting to different situations.

Anonymous: The Social Organism

To properly describe Anonymous, the world of 4chan must first be described. 4chan, founded in 2003, is an internet imageboard where anything goes.[1] There are over 50 different categories of boards within the website, the most popular of which is the random board, also known as /b/. No registration is required to post on /b/, or any other of the boards. Thus, all posts on the site are posted under the alias "Anonymous". The lack of censorship, combined with the ability to post anonymously, provided a fertile womb for the formation and birth of the collective Anonymous.

Anonymous was born as the shared identity[2] of those who enjoyed the Lulz, which is a pluralized form of the acronym LOL (laugh out loud).[3] The collective would congregate on the imageboard, sharing material with each other. Some posts are clever and funny material, while others are vulgar and tasteless. If the Anons (someone who is part of Anonymous) enjoy a particular thread, it will thrive and many people will contriboot (purposeful misspelling of contribute). On the contrary, if fellow Anons view a thread with disdain, they will call OP (original poster) a fag and find a way to derail the thread. A common method of derailing is posting many different pictures of Spiderman with text saying things like, "I'm taking control of this thread" or "What's that? A Spidey thread?" This mentality has remained throughout the evolution of Anonymous.

Anonymous is no longer only about the Lulz. It has grown and matured. Anons still enjoy their Lulz, but it has become about much more now.[4] It has grown from being young and immature, to being seasoned and morally-guided. This process began with a squabble between Anonymous and the Church of Scientology. When a Tom Cruise propaganda video leaked from the church, Scientologists were furious and demanded it be removed from the internet. Their persistence was the foot that kicked the hornet's nest. Anonymous swarmed the church through DDoS attacks, prank calls, and black faxes. The attack on the Church of Scientology was a mixture of the pursuit of Lulz and a new side of Anonymous that had yet to be seen, the side that was actually serious. However, for Anons the act of being serious is never completely free of humor. This conflict, known as Project Chanology, also marked the first time that the Anon identity took physical form. People took to the streets for protests against the church. This marked the turning point of the masked collective.

---

[1] http://www.4chan.org

[2] Tivona, Devon. "We Are Anonymous: Noble Freedom Fighters or Cyber Terrorists? The Colorado Engineer." The Colorado Engineer. January 23, 2012. Accessed April 26, 2012. http://cem.colorado.edu/?p=163.

[3] Norton, Quinn. "Anonymous 101: Introduction to the Lulz." Wired.com. November 08, 2011. Accessed April 26, 2012. http://www.wired.com/threatlevel/2011/11/anonymous-101/all/1.

[4] Norton, Quinn. "Anonymous 101 Part Deux: Morals Triumph Over Lulz." Wired.com. December 30, 2011. Accessed April 26, 2012. http://www.wired.com/threatlevel/2011/12/anonymous-101-part-deux/?utm_source=Contextly.

The Social Organism

As a social organism, Anonymous was born of 4chan, spent its youth messing around, and matured into a conscious full-grown body. Common knowledge says that for a body to survive, certain functions must work properly. Just as in the human body, there is a brain, digestive system, and immune system that help the collective continue to flourish.

The Brain

The brain of anonymous has multiple functions. First, is the idea behind Anonymous. It is that part of the collective that makes it what it is. Second, is the decision making process. It is the part that guides the Anons and determines what is worthy of the brand.

The idea behind Anonymous is not simple to describe. It is a leaderless collective, with no hermetic ideology. It may not subscribe to any religion, but it does have its principles.[5] Summarizing anything about succinctly is a difficult task, but their principles seem to be all come down to the same thing, freedom. For Anonymous freedom includes the freedom of speech and information. These freedoms are viewed as the means to their end. The goals that are pursued are social justice, the betterment of society, and achieving a truly democratic society. Anything that infringes on these freedoms or prevents these goals becomes an enemy. This includes corrupt governments, greedy corporations, and all forms of censorship. The internet is viewed as their home, a place where ideas can flourish and authority can be challenged. Therefore, anything that tries to stop this becomes a target. However, it is important to remember that the Lulz always remain important.

The decision making in Anonymous is similar to the way in which threads become successful on /b/. Operations are suggested daily in Anon nation, yet few ever grab hold. For an operation to be successful and gain support it must present a cause and some possible solutions that a large number of Anons agree with. An attempt to harness Anonymous as a personal army will get rejected, but a worthy cause will often gather a great deal of support. This decision making process must be understood as horizontalist, which means that there is no hierarchy. In the decision making process, no one opinion is more important than the next. This form of decision making is an accurate representation of the population involved. Operations are only carried out if the majority of people agree with the suggestion, and dissenters are not obligated to participate.

The Circulatory System

The circulatory system functions as a distribution system throughout the body of Anonymous. Fast and effective communication is critical for the collective. For this reason, the form of communication used depends on its purpose. Widespread news about Anonymous, or anything that pertains to their interest, is distributed via social networks. Both Facebook and Twitter have

---

[5] http://knowyourmeme.com/memes/rules-of-the-internet

multiple accounts that perform this function. Another "mainstream" source is YouTube, which is often used to deliver a message to the enemy or to call Anons to action. Links to these messages are often posted on social networks.

Other forms are used for more direct communication among specific groups. A popular method is Internet Relay Chat (IRC). An IRC is basically an instant messaging chat room, in which a group can congregate and communicate. They are usually not encrypted or password protected, so anyone who has access to the url can join the chat. VoxAnon[6] is a great example of an IRC that facilitates communication among Anons. It has various channels with different purposes. There are channels for new Anons, which are sometimes referred to as "newfags." There are also other channels to discuss certain operations. Although a majority of the time the conversations are pointless, a lot can be accomplished on the IRCs when the right group is brought together

As the name suggests, anonymity is important to Anonymous. Thus, it becomes essential at times for participants to mask their identity when communicating or carrying out operations. A favorite form of concealing identities is a program called TOR (the onion router). TOR operates by sending an encrypted link through a series of random nodes that then deliver an unencrypted link to the desired recipient. This process makes it extremely difficult for an outside source to trace the user's actions. Other proxies are used, but TOR seems to reign supreme.

The Immune System

Anonymous considers itself to be an all-inclusive group. Everyone in this world, who is oppressed, censored, victimized by injustice, or just concerned with any of these is a part of the identity[7]. Therefore, if anyone is victimized, censored, or oppressed, the whole body of Anonymous feels the effects. This is where the immune system kicks in. It sees the infection of injustice and sends in the antibodies to fight the problem.

The antibodies of Anonymous are the operations. Many operations are embarked on. Some receive media attention, some are known primarily by those who follow Anonymous, and some of the smaller operations go largely unnoticed. Some of the more well-known operations have been Project Chanology, OpBart, and OpDarknet[8]. Each of these examples shows a different facet of Anonymous. Project Chanology as previously discussed was the birth of the conscience of Anonymous. OpBart is a good example of what followed. It was in response to Bay Area Rapid Transport system shutting down cell phone service in their stations in anticipation of protests. The protests were planned in

---

[6] www.voxanon.org

[7] Fantz, Ashley. "Who Is Anonymous? Everyone and No One." CNN. February 09, 2012. Accessed April 26, 2012. http://articles.cnn.com/2012-02-09/world/world_anonymous-explainer_1_chat-room-internet-caf-anonymous-members?_s=PM:WORLD.

[8] http://pastebin.com/u/opdarknet

response to the police killing a man, Oscar Grant, in one of the stations. In this operation Anons hacked and defaced myBART.org, took to the streets, and raised awareness to the issue.

OpDarknet shows an interesting side of Anonymous. In this case, it is Anonymous that did the censoring. Within the TOR program, hidden child pornography sites called Hard Candy and Lolita City were discovered. Warnings were issued to the administrators of the site, but they were ignored. The collective then took action against the perpetrators by cooperating with the Mozilla foundation (developer of Firefox). In collaboration, they created the HoneyPawt which replaced the TOR program. This replacement enabled the actors in this operation to log the IP addresses of users that attempted to access the child pornography sites. The IP addresses were released to the public, along with a map to display the location of the IP addresses. The websites were then disabled using continuous denial-of-service attacks. This shows that even the outspoken voice of free speech is willing to put limits on what is allowed on the internet.

Different operations require different methods. As they did in OpDarknet, Anonymous often uses denial-of-service (DDoS) attacks on the enemies. DDoS attacks temporarily shut down websites by sending a huge amount of requests at once. They do this through Low-Orbit Ion Cannon (LOIC), which enables single users to send multiple requests to a website at one time. When a lot of people do this, it leads to a server crashing. Along with DDoS attacks, the collective also participates in hacking, although this is usually carried out by a specific sect of Anonymous. The hacking usually consists of defacing websites and stealing information. Sometimes however, the collective mind of Anonymous is not enough in itself to carry out an operation successfully. When this is the case, the collective turns to outside partnerships such as the Occupy movement, Wikileaks, and Mozilla. This also expands the ranks of Anonymous and leads to the battle stepping off the computer screen and into the streets.

Conclusion

The concept of Anonymous can be difficult to comprehend. It has to be understood as a collective identity of all the individuals that agree with it, even in part. Any activism that fights injustice could be considered a part of Anonymous. In a way it is a humanist movement taking its own form. It is an idea that has manifested itself and taken a life of its own. For this reason, it should be understood as a social organism. It has a brain, a digestive system, and an immune system. These perform the same function as they would in a living organism, just in a different way. It is through these functions that Anonymous stays alive and continues to make a difference.

Bibliography

Fantz, Ashley. "Who Is Anonymous? Everyone and No One." CNN. February

09, 2012. Accessed April 26, 2012. http://articles.cnn.com/2012-02-09/world/world_anonymous-explainer_1_chat-room-internet-caf-anonymous-members?_s=PM:WORLD.

Norton, Quinn. "Anonymous 101: Introduction to the Lulz." Wired.com. November 08, 2011. Accessed April 26, 2012. http://www.wired.com/threatlevel/2011/11/anonymous-101/all/1.

Norton, Quinn. "Anonymous 101 Part Deux: Morals Triumph Over Lulz." Wired.com. December 30, 2011. Accessed April 26, 2012. http://www.wired.com/threatlevel/2011/12/anonymous-101-part-deux/?utm_source=Contextly.

Tivona, Devon. "We Are Anonymous: Noble Freedom Fighters or Cyber Terrorists? The Colorado Engineer." The Colorado Engineer. January 23, 2012. Accessed April 26, 2012. http://cem.colorado.edu/?p=163.

Identifying Anonymous

Jackie Pittaway

Anonymous began on the imageboard 4chan. It began as a meme, evolved into a culture and morphed into a network. Anonymous is a spontaneous collective of people who share a common goal of protecting the free flow of information, yet even this assertion cannot be verified by the very nature of Anonymous where no one person can speak for them, but the users that make up Anonymous do have a code of ethics and culture that applies to them across the board. In 2008 Anonymous morphed from a bunch of internet crusaders to politically minded activists. For simplicities sake, Anonymous will be referred to as they. That does not mean that what is being presented is something every member of Anonymous agrees to, rather it is a view that a prominent member or a majority of Anonymous adhere to. One thing that all of Anonymous can agree on is the importance of free flow of information. Presently the free flow of information is the most important issue to Anonymous.

The image most associated with Anonymous is the Guy Fawkes mask. Most people believe the mask is a reference to the movie "V for Vendetta" which is not the case. The Guy Fawkes mask came from the Epic Fail Guy meme. The Epic Fail Guy meme originated on the imageboard 4chan in late 2006. Epic Fail Guy originally came without the mask. He would inevitably fail at everything he tried to do. On September 30th, 2008 Epic Fail Guy found a Guy Fawkes mask when he stuck his head in a trashcan to look closer at something in the trashcan. From then on Epic Fail Guy almost always wears the Guy Fawkes mask. When Anonymous challenged the Church of Scientology over the take down of a YouTube video mocking Tom Cruise they took to the streets wearing Guy Fawkes mask. The mask was not a reference to the ending of "V for Vendetta," instead it was a commentary on how much of a failure the Church of Scientology is (Knowyourmeme.com).

The meaning behind the mask changed as the nature of Anonymous changed. Another more practical reason the mask is used is for safety reasons. Anonymous urged the protesters to mask their identity to avoid being targeted by the Church of Scientology and later, other more powerful targets. Wearing the mask became a matter of privacy and safety. A fairly prominent member of Anonymous that went by the pseudonym Topiary was quoted saying," Revolution is a horde of activists holding up Anonymous masks and thanking us for assisting their hard work by obliterating their government's ministry, stock and finance websites, replacing them with inspiring words. Revolution, to me, is bringing down the big guy while not forgetting to stand up for the little guy" (Christian Science Monitor). Lulz no longer motivate Anonymous, instead the end goal is revolution. Formerly, Anonymous would instigate raids as a means of entertainment or for some minor moral reason such as power abuse by moderators, but now Anonymous is happy to attack those who violate the principles which they stand for. They have embraced the role of V in "V for Vendetta." Anonymous actively seeks to protect the rights of people who have no idea their rights are being violated and they seek to show complacent people that they need to stand up to big government and corporations if they want to be free. The remarkable thing is that Anonymous has developed principles. They are few, but they exist. Anonymous went from being a group of online marauders to internet vigilantes.

Anonymous has developed a set of guidelines they adhere to. Anonymous believes that only legitimate power comes from the consent of the governed. The government can control those it governs by controlling information, but if power is derived from consent of the governed then the governed need to be able to access information. A corrupt government is one that withholds information from its people. The governed need to be able to make informed decisions. Vital to making good decisions is access to information. Anonymous values free flow of information above all else. They do what they do "so your voice may never be silenced" (Commander X). Anonymous initiated Operation Bahrain, an attempt to effect change a government that they see as a dictatorship, based on this belief (Weaver). Freedom of speech and access to information is sacred to a group where nothing is sacred. Protecting freedom of speech means protecting the press. Anonymous, while distrustful of mainstream media, absolutely will not attack the press. Internal guidelines for Anonymous include anti-egoism and anti-fame sentiments (Coleman). While Topiary feels rewarded by the activists gratitude Anonymous is not about self recognition. Those who seek it are attacked by others. Similarly, one of Anonymous' important rules is that they are not your personal army. What this means is Anonymous is not a tool to pursue your personal vendettas. Though their rules are few and far between, Anonymous does have a set of rules that they follow and certain principles that they value.

Anonymous still insists that the lulz are its primary motivation, but they have come to acknowledge that they are more than just a bunch of guys hanging out on the internet together causing trouble. According to the members of Anonymous, Anonymous does not exist. It is not a person or a thing; it's an internet meme that can be appropriated by anyone for any cause. However, even this extremely broad open interpretation is subject to restrictions. Anonymous cannot be an individual. No one person can take the name of Anonymous and apply it to their own cause. For instance, The Guardian published an article concerning a man who planned to publish the details of women who had abortions (Pearse). This man is not Anonymous, though he was a member of anonymous his actions were unsupported by others. He acted alone. In order for an action to be carried out by Anonymous the action must be put to a majority vote. Not all raids are successful, raids that do not get a following do not get carried out. Anonymous also relies on Distributed Denial of Service attacks for most of their raids. DDOS attacks require a large number of participants to succeed. For a raid to be approved a member must put an idea out on to the Internet Relay Chat, a fairly old way of chatting online, and if other members approve it they set a date for the raid and anyone who wants to participate joins the designated IRC and opens their computer up to join in the DDOS attacks.

The raids fail when not enough people participate as with the raids on Tumblr and Facebook, but when they get enough supporters they can generate enough requests to take down government sites (Coleman).

Under the advice of "wise beard man," a former member of the Church at Scientology, some members of Anonymous have chosen to revise their methods of getting what they want. Mark Bunker, wise beard man, told Anonymous that to be taken seriously they needed to legitimize which mean giving up illegal DDOS attacks. Some members of Anonymous strictly adhere to this. Those who operate through whyweprotest.net are among the members who refuse to use DDOS, instead they use legal means such as making YouTube videos, writing letters or getting on a radio program (Whyweprotest.net). Anonymous has branched off into different groups who try to accomplish the same goals through different means. Those who do use DDOS argue that it is a form of civil disobedience. DDOS attacks do not physically harm anyone and can be used to raise awareness. The aim of the attacks is to protect the free flow of information and hold the government accountable for its actions (Wikileaks, 87). The uniting factor for these different groups is the desire to protect rights. Anyone can join Anonymous and the people who participate in the operations are not always the same people. Gabriella Coleman, assistant Professor of Media, Culture and Communication at Steinhardt, argues that in order to successfully be a member of Anonymous one must use IRC and blend with the culture (Coleman).

The turning point for Anonymous came when they began to attack the Church of Scientology because of a violation of freedom of speech rather than amusement. Prior to these attacks Anonymous would go on small scale moral raids and anyone who was seen as a do gooder was called a moralfag. Anonymous originally stuck to small raids such as the Habbo raids. Anonymous would attack Habbo, a social networking site, over mod abuse (Wikipedia). Once Anonymous got involved with the Church of Scientology they began to transition from small scale raids to larger raids motivated by the desire to protect rights rather than doing it for the lulz. The Church of Scientology also marks the first time that Anonymous manifested physically rather than over forums or IRC. Anonymous has continued to grow and to take themselves more seriously. After the takedown of Megaupload by the United States Government Anonymous created their own file sharing network (Anonyupload.com). After Google+ refused to allow Anonymous to create a page, saying they do not support the activities of Anonymous, Anonymous members got to work creating AnonPlus. What is particularly remarkable about AnonPlus is that on the image they are using as place holder until the site is done they say, "Welcome to the Revolution . . . We have arrived" (Anonplus.com). The mantra of Anonymous is "We do not forgive, we do not forget, expect us." By saying they have arrived, this particular sect has moved Anonymous out of the threatening stage and into an active stage where they are following through on their promises and actively trying to bring about revolutions. Commander X, a member of Anonymous who has led operations, stresses that Anonymous past is not its present. The Anonymous that carried out the Habbo raids is not the Anonymous that has allied itself with Wikileaks. Commander X describes Anonymous as a living idea that can be changed anytime. Anonymous has changed significantly since its inception and have grown to the point that they can and will take action to achieve their goals.

Anonymous has its very own Declaration of Independence which is remarkable in that it claims Anonymous as a state. The Declaration of /b/ Independence came about after the members of Anonymous were outraged by what they perceived as mod abuse. The declaration, written by Captain Cornflake, separated Anonymous from 4chan. In the declaration they claim the Anonymous states of /b/ "out to be a Free and Independent State . . . they have full Power to levy War, conclude Peace contract Alliances, establish Commerce, and to do all other Acts and Things which Independent States may of right do." They frequently use the power to levy war when they coordinate their operations and declare war on companies like PayPal. They also have made alliances with organizations such as Wikileaks and aided protesters in Tunisia and Egypt. Once a target has acquiesced to the demands of Anonymous they conclude peace which was also done with PayPal (The Lurkmore Wiki).

The structure of Anonymous is such that there is no leader and it can never be shut down, except from within. Anonymous is very much a hivemind. They are a beehive without a queen. There are no leaders, only prominent members, in the sense that they are highly visible and participate frequently and take on larger roles in organizing operations. Anonymous lacks structure and hierarchy. All it takes to be in Anonymous is show up at the right IRC channels and participate. Anonymous is what Paul Mason, author of Why it's Kicking-off Everywhere, calls a network. A network is a loosely bound group of people connected via internet or social networking. A network has no structure, no leader and can't be shut down because of its loosely organized nature. The network Mason describes is one capable of eroding traditional power relationships. Networks give power to those who were traditionally at a disadvantage. Networks enable the rapid spread of information. Anonymous fits the bill well (Mason, 80).

There are strengths and weaknesses to the nature of a network. As previously mentioned a network cannot be shut down. Anonymous is so large with so many members and so many platforms that taking out perceived leaders or shutting down a group like Lulzsec will not end Anonymous. They will just reform and come back for more. The problem with the loose nature of Anonymous is that it is easy to walk away from. This is what Malcolm Gladwell calls weak ties. Weak ties reduce commitment needed to join the cause. While networks enable for instantaneous mass action, they also allow people to walk away just as quickly as they came (Mason, 81). Gladwell is of the opinion that to effect real change one must be part of a hierarchy. Mason points out that there are other ways to challenge a traditional hierarchy than working through the system. When at a disadvantage, the underdogs can use swarm tactics. Anonymous effectively uses low tech swarm tactics to accomplish their goals. The Low Orbit Ion Canon is not particularly complicated or high tech, but it is highly effective when enough people participate. Another problem Gladwell recognizes is that a network must be interested in systematic change if anything is to be accomplished, groups that are just interested in getting noticed do not accomplish anything. Anonymous falls into both of those categories. They desire change in governments and have an idea about how they want to do it, but they way they seek to accomplish change is through drawing attention with DDOS attacks and defacing government websites. While they certainly do draw attention their success rate for actually effecting change varies (Mason 82). Anonymous has successfully pressured PayPal into changing their policy and they have facilitated revolutions throughout the Middle East and Tunisia, but for every successful operations there are multiple failed operations. However, it cannot be ignored that Anonymous has successfully held corporations responsible for their actions. As a network Anonymous has found success with corporations, but if they hope to change governments as their attacks on China and the FBI websites indicate they will need a bit more structure and organization.

Anonymous is difficult to understand because of its fluid nature. Members come and go and no one is vital to running Anonymous. Anonymous lacks structure and there are very few things members have in common. The only thing they hold sacred is the free flow of information. Anonymous has changed from what it once was and may yet change again. Anonymous has shown that it can effect change and it will fight to protect the rights of people all over the world. Anonymous has turned into a moralfag.

Bibliography

Boone, Jeb. "By teaming with Wikileaks, Anonymous gains in notoriety | GlobalPost." World News | Breaking US News and International News Headlines - GlobalPost. N.p., 12 Feb. 2012. Web. 17 Apr. 2012. <www.globalpost.com/dispatches/globalpost-blogs/the-grid/anonymous-wikileaks>.

Bright, Arthur. "6 men alleged to be LulzSec hackers - Jake Davis, alleged to be 'Topiary' - CSMonitor.com." The Christian Science Monitor - CSMonitor.com. N.p., n.d. Web. 17 Apr. 2012. <http://www.csmonitor.com/World/Global-Issues/2012/0308/The-6-men-alleged-   to-be-   LulzSec-hackers>.

Coleman, Gabriella . "Anonymous: From the Lulz to Collective Action | The New Everyday." MediaCommons | a digital scholarly network. N.p., n.d. Web. 28 Feb. 2012. <http://mediacommons.futureofthebook.org/tne/pieces/anonymous-lulz-collective-action>.

Coleman, Gabriella . "What It's Like to Participate in Anonymous' Actions - Gabriella Coleman - Technology - The Atlantic." The Atlantic — News and analysis on politics, business, culture, technology, national, international, and life, TheAtlantic.com. N.p., 10 Dec. 2010. Web. 28 Feb. 2012. <http://www.theatlantic.com/technology/archive/2010/12/what-its-like-to-participate-in-anonymous-actions/67860/>.

Mason, Paul. Why it's Kicking Off Everywhere: The New Global Revolutions. London: Verso 2012.

Pearse, Damien. " Anonymous hacker planned to publish details of women who had abortions | UK news | guardian.co.uk ." Latest US news, world news, sport and comment from the Guardian | guardiannews.com |. 10 Mar. 2012. Web. 17 Apr. 2012. <http://www.guardian.co.uk/uk/2012/mar/10/anonymous-hacker-women-abortion>.

Weaver, Paul. "Bahrain unrest 'nothing to do with us', says F1 chief Bernie Ecclestone | World news | The Guardian ." The Guardian . N.p., n.d. Web. 26 Apr. 2012. <http://www.guardian.co.uk/world/2012/apr/20/bahrain-unrest-f1-bernie-ecclestone>.

X, Commander. "Day Of Rage - Occupy Wall Street - Anonymous on Vimeo." Vimeo, Video Sharing For You. N.p., n.d. Web. 17 Apr. 2012. <http://vimeo.com/29235898>.

"Anonyupload - Download any files anytime, anywhere! It's Free, Legal & Nice !." Anonyupload - Download any files anytime, anywhere! It's Free, Legal & Nice!. N.p., n.d. Web. 28 Feb. 2012. <http://www.anonyupload.com/>.

"Brian Lehrer Live with Gabriella Coleman (TV interview on anonymous) - YouTube ." YouTube - Broadcast Yourself. . N.p., n.d. Web. 28 Feb. 2012. <http://www.youtube.com/watch?v=TGsoRd8jwfM>.

"Operation Payback Manifesto." AnonNews.org : Everything Anonymous. N.p., n.d. Web. 17 Apr. 2012. <http://anonnews.org/press/item/36/>.

"Timeline of events associated with Anonymous - Wikipedia, the free encyclopedia." Wikipedia,   the free encyclopedia. N.p., n.d. Web. 17 Apr. 2012. <http://en.wikipedia.org/wiki/Timeline_of_events_involving_Anonymous>.

"The Declaration of /b/ Independence." The LURKMORE Wiki. N.p., n.d. Web. 28 Feb. 2012. <http://www.lurkmore.com/wiki/Anony>

"What is Anonymous? - Understand Us! - YouTube ." YouTube - Broadcast Yourself. . N.p., n.d. Web. 17 Apr. 2012. <http://www.youtube.com/watch?v=7cqP8qqqfI0&feature=related>.

Anonymous is Not One Person

Richard Redford

Anonymous is not one person, several people directed by one person, or a group of people directed by several people. Rather, Anonymous is more like an idea, an idea that has become accepted by a versatile collection of primarily internet oriented users. It is important to understand that Anonymous has no permanent leader(s) and performs operations utilizing a virtually horizontal power structure. All operations are critically discussed beforehand via Internet Relay Chat, otherwise known as IRC. IRC plays an important role for the group; allowing on demand communication and coordination to take place. As a result, Distributed Denial of Service attacks are easily coordinated, as well as other pranks designed to cause mayhem such as for example, perpetual unwarranted telephone calls and unpaid pizza deliveries. Anonymous enjoys mayhem, but in order to understand why, one must understand the make-up of the core values of Anonymous

Anonymous was founded for reasons of creating mayhem and to having fun. From the beginning: exciting pranks and trickery have been the norms of Anonymous' intention. Anonymous defines its motivation as the Lulz. To understand Anonymous, one must first understand this concept of the Lulz. The Lulz is the spine of Anonymous. The Lulz acts as the core stimulus for any action members of the group decide to take. By definition, the Lulz is a variation of the acronym LOL. In internet jargon, LOL is an acronym short for: laugh out loud. Lulz may be defined as a type of dark and painful humor. According to an article by wired.com journalist Quinn Norton titled, Anonymous 101: Introduction to the Lulz, "The Lulz is laughing instead of screaming. It's [a] laughter of embarrassment and separation... it's humor that heightens contradictions... [It's] laughter with pain in it." The Lulz is a strategy of humor and mayhem in a world where power is everything. Ultimately, it represents the core motivational force of Anonymous. The Lulz is the intention of the culture that is Anonymous.

In early January 2008, a video of Tom Cruise went viral. The video depicted an enthusiastic Cruise praising the theology of the Church of Scientology. The video itself appeared on several video hosting sites, mainly YouTube, Gawker, and Defaner. In an apparent attempt to take control of the leaked video situation, the Church swiftly issued threats of legal action if the video was not immediately removed. Threatened with a potential Copyright lawsuit, the sites removed the video. However, the video was never removed for long. Soon after its removal, another copy would be uploaded by another user. The video had effectively gone viral. When the information was made public that the Church of Scientology was attempting to remove the Tom Cruise video from the public domain, Anonymous became infuriated. On IRC, it was decided that because of an attempted suppression of speech, as well as a history of silencing critics, the Church was guilty of feeding the trolls. As a result, the hive mind of Anonymous declared war Project Chanology was born.

According to Anonymous, the Church of Scientology was guilty of feeding the trolls. Feeding the trolls meant Anonymous had a reason to attack the Church. It meant the beginning of a string of raids. The leaked video of Tom Cruise however was not enough to start the war. It was the Church's suppression and attempted censorship of the Video itself that truly fed the appetite of the Anonymous hive. This apparent attack on free speech fueled Anonymous to take action and declare war on the Church of Scientology. The Church was feeding Anonymous' desire to create mayhem. And mayhem is what fuels the fires of Anonymous' excitement. At first Anonymous did not care much about the alleged human rights abuses conducted by the Church. Anonymous was more focused on the fun it would have destroying it.

But what exactly is the Church of Scientology? American science fiction writer L. Ron Hubbard, author of the book Dianetics, founded the Church of Scientology in 1952. Scientology teaches that all human beings are immortal Thetans, or spirits. Thetans can never die and thus when the physical body is destroyed, the spirit itself lives on. As a result, Scientologist's believe that humans have lived many different physical lives and overtime we have forgotten our true nature. In order to become spiritually rehabilitated, Scientology offers a service called auditing. Auditing is a type of listening exercise, where the person, who is listening, known as the auditor, helps restore the true nature of the practitioner. The auditor utilizes a special machine known as an E-meter. An E-meter measures electrical conductance expressed by a person's skin. The E-meter is held by the practitioner, while the auditor asks questions and observes the electrical skin conductance meter. Scientologist's claim that the electrical conductance of the E-meter reflects whether or not a person has overcome the negative energies of painful past experience.

But what's with all the controversy? First of all, in the United States, the Church of Scientology is a legally recognized religion. Thus, the Church enjoys a tax-exempt status while enjoying a hefty income of over one hundred million dollars annually. Where does this money come from? Ex-scientologist's claim that it takes an estimated four hundred thousand dollars in auditing fees in order to graduate into the higher levels of the church. Secondly, the Church of Scientology is known to practice a policy called "Fair Game". Fair Game policy authorizes the Church to harass any and all critics as well as Church defectors by any means possible. This policy has been claimed by the Church to be a sacred religious right, a core religious belief of the Church. This religious policy of Fair Gaming has led to a series of mysterious deaths; including suicides, stabbings, and instances of torture. Moreover, many ex-scientologists claim to have feared for their life when publicly considering leaving the Church. Moreover, hundreds of children are born into the church. These children rarely if ever see their parents, are sheltered from anything that is not Scientology, and are reportedly subject to harsh labor conditions. It is important to understand however that what truly drew Anonymous' attention was not necessarily the Church's critics—at least at first. Rather, what pushed Anonymous' buttons was the Church's ruthless attacks of censorship.

As a result of Scientology's Censoring tactics, the first wave of Project Chanology raids began. The first wave of raids lasted from January 15th to the 27th. According to Quinn Norton, these raids consisted of: "making creepy phone calls, phoning in fake pizza deliveries, sending threatening emails, faxing black pages of paper to waste toner [and] overloading servers...Classic online troll fare." Anonymous acted in a manner to be expected; causing mayhem in an effort to get a rise out of the Church because they thought it was funny. Motivated by the Lulz, Anonymous released several videos declaring war on the Church of Scientology. Five days after the Lulzy declaration of war, anti-Scientology activist Mark Bunker pleaded with the Anon's to renounce their trollish ways. Unknowingly, Mark Bunker would provide the needed spark necessary for Anonymous' "moral' evolution.

Mark Bunker became known to Anonymous as the Wise Beard Man, "his words are wise, his face is beard." Bunker spoke directly to the Anon's asking them to legitimize their demonstrations against the Church. He called for an end to distributed denial of service attacks and a shift to a more serious legal protest movement. Mark Bunker's appeal triggered a string of heated debates in IRC. Many old-school Anon's viewed any type of intentional morality as a corruption of the Lulz. These members became known as the 'oldfags'. As Norton explains, "They were supposed to be taking down the church for the Lulz, and righteous vigilantism was just meant to be part of the joke." The oldfags argued that morality was never meant to be part of the motivation. However, a high enough majority of the hive found the concept of moral vigilantism appealing. Anonymous decided to enter the Meat Space. The Meat Space is another word for physical reality. Eventually, enough Anons agreed and decided to take the Project Chanology raids to the next level. Anonymous decided to leave the internet for the first time.

Over IRC, Anonymous set up the time, date, and location for the protest. On February 10, 2008, Anonymous showed up in front of Scientology churches around the world. In all, over 6,000 people, sporting Guy Fawkes masks and carrying signs attended the protests. But these protests were quite unique. Overwhelmingly motivated by the Lulz, the protests resembled more of a party than a politically conscious protest movement. According to Quinn Norton, "[Protestors] played music and walked around with signs that both accused Scientology of crimes and referenced obscure internet memes." However, soon many Anons receded from the Meat Space back onto the internet. And yet at the same time, many Anons chose to remain and continue to organize protests as of a Los Angeles protest dated March 17, 2012. Those members who continue to protest tend to focus on awareness of the alleged human rights abuses of the Church of Scientology. To support Scientology abuse and protest awareness,

Anonymous is not one person

Anons have also created the website whyweprotest.net. This website contains easy to access material outlining the purpose of Project Chanology. The site also provides an active community forum that is used for discussion as well as for protest coordination.

An Irish Anon protester is quoted as saying, "I came for the Lulz, but I stayed for the outrage." Ultimately, the Lulz has never disappeared from what can be defined as the political subgroup of Anonymous. Politically active Anons continue to utilize the Lulz as a means of Unity and Release. The intention of the Lulz itself continues to link members of Anonymous in a sort of commonality. At the same time, the Lulz has become a release valve for many politically active members. According to Gabriella Coleman, the Lulz "makes the hard and sometimes depressing work of political engagement more bearable. As Anonymous becomes increasingly political, members have found the importance of practicing a balance between acting in terms of morality and keeping with the intention of the Lulz. This balancing act has become integrated into the political subgroups of Anonymous.

As a result of Project Chanology, Anonymous continues to evolve and develop subgroups of politically conscious Operations. The creation and ultimate success of Operations such as Op Tunisia and Op Payback represent a direct result of the Impact Project Chanology has had on Anonymous as a culture. Because of Project Chanology, the doctrine of the Lulz was further examined and allowed to be incorporated within a politically conscious movement. As a result, Anonymous has become a gateway for internet users to become politically active. As Gabriella Coleman states, "The decision to engage in political action has to happen somehow, via a concrete path of action, a set of events, or influences; Anonymous is precisely that path for many. Ultimately, Project Chanology marks the origin for the birth of political consciousness within the culture known as Anonymous and has become a pathway for political change.

References

Norton, Quinn. *Anonymous 101: Introduction to the Lulz. Wired.com*. 8 Nov. 2011. Web. 10 Apr. 2012.

Coleman, Gabriella. *Anonymous -- From Lulz to a Collective.*
Http://www.thenewsignificance.com/. 9 May 2011. Web. 10 Apr. 2012.
<http://www.thenewsignificance.com/2011/05/09/gabriella-coleman-anonymous-from-the-lulz-to-collective-action/>.

Why WeProtest. Anonymous. Web. 4 Apr. 2012. <http://whyweprotest.net>.

Legal Responses to Anonymous

Austin Rogers

Being an International hactivist group has opened up Anonymous to numerous responses by both legal entities and even by a Sinaloa Drug cartel. Anonymous has faced responses from local governments, Congress, and even the Church of Scientology: and that's just in the United States This section will detail the responses taken in San Francisco due to the BART protests, the response of the Church of Scientology, the attempts by the FBI to shut down Anonymous (namely the LULZSEC) and the consequences of its international attacks in Mexico.

Project Chanology was an Anonymous led cyber attack in 2008 on the Church of Scientology for perceived freedom of speech violations and it alleged that the Church coerced YouTube in to removing a potentially damaging interview with actor Tom Cruise. A news report by the British newspaper The Guardian detailed the attacks, "Guerrilla action has so far included the temporary disabling of its international website and "Google bombing", a manipulation of the search engine which has resulted in the website being the first result returned by Google when users type "dangerous cult". (Barkham). Such attacks were responded to by the Church through both through legal and public relations channels. After these cyber attacks could not be stopped The Church sought the FBI's help in stopping Anonymous. While this response did net a few arrests in the form of a few on the street protestors it failed in stopping the larger "LulzSec" and Anonymous in general. The Church of Scientology came out to the media to publically denounce Anonymous. While an official spokesperson said, "We are taking action, Anonymous will be handled and stopped, but not to the detriment of us stopping all community outreach activities. We've had people throw attacks at us in the past as they do not agree with the betterment of people. History is strewn with such people who start wars, wreak havoc etc. and they never continue to exist in the long run as their purpose is one of destruction. That's a statistical and historical fact", (Church) they also appeared on syndicated television shows and were quoted as referring to Anonymous as goon, thugs, and pigs". (Church).

This attack and subsequent response was an important turning point for Anonymous as it was just in its infancy when Project Chanology began. This was also seen by the online community as a "War on the Internet". In this "war" the two sides of Scientology and Anonymous both used attacks on each other to try and win favor. In spite of attempts by the Church to portray Anonymous negatively 88% of a WikiNews pool believed that Anonymous would win. The media barrage by the Church also brought national attention to Anonymous that would otherwise not have been available. Until Project Chanology Anonymous only really existed to those who frequented, the oft obscene 4chan website. Post operation Chanology Anonymous had many new followers and garnered national attention for future attacks. The Church of Scientology on the other hand has faded into the background and has received criticism from the mass media for its practices. This also marks a victory for the legal protests advocated by "wise beard man". Prior to the successful protests Anons had been using illegal DDOS attacks to accomplish their agenda and this marked the first time Anonymous was successful through legal means.

One of the first times Anonymous forayed into the physical world was on August 15th 2011. This attack was in response to actions taken by Bay Area Rapid Transit officials to block cell phone service to disrupt a planned protest on August 11th for a BART police related shooting earlier in the year (McMillan) Even prior to the June shooting of Oscar Grant in cold blood the BART police had been notorious for abuse of power and the shooting of a detained man in police custody only intensified the disdain for this non-governmental police force. The protest of BART police practices was registered and approved by the city of San Francisco and its aim was to bring about awareness for the injustice of the verdict (Involuntary Manslaughter). Seeking to stop organizers from organizing. This disruption was viewed as necessary to protect the evening commute by BART but Anonymous saw this as violation of basic First Amendments Right's. After Anonymous's #OpBarts second protest police began arresting the protestors. The San Francisco police cited that the protestors' high volume and use of noise amplifiers created a dangerous situation on the platform and the removal of protestors by force was necessary to protect public safety, "Last night when BART police witnessed what they deemed to be criminal activity they made arrests. All protesters detained on the BART platform were arrested under Section 369i of the California Penal Code, which states that anyone who interferes with the safe and efficient operation of a train is guilty of a misdemeanor. At least one or two were using amplified devices to shout on the platform level, which creates a dangerous situation." (Morris).

The response by BART is significant because along with this being the first Anonymous held protest it also marks the first time "real world" actions taken under the flag of Anonymous resulted in police action and arrests. The show of support by the civilian populace and the coverage of the arrests led to an increased profile that would prove invaluable as the Occupy movement began only a month after the BART protests and with the strong support of Anonymous the San Francisco Bay Area has been a key battleground for that movement. Currently the protests still rage within San Francisco and in early April a man on the tracks actually stopped service temporarily.

Up until late 2011 Anonymous had really only attacked legal enterprises and thus had left alone the more shady business world of violent gangs. This all changed in late October 2011 when Anonymous declared #opcartel. The purpose of #Opcartel was to expose those officials in Mexico and Central America who were known to be corrupted by the influence of one of the largest criminal conglomerates in the world, the Zetas. Anonymous claimed that the passage of the Mexican SOPA which "proposed law that will see those who violate copyright online fined one million pesos (over $100,000)"(Anonymous) is a violation of international free speech and was being passed by corrupt politicians who do not act in the best interests of their people.

The proposed action was highly divisive within the Anonymous camp. Reuters reported that Mexican Anon's "didn't want to touch it with a 10 foot pole and even others did not want to incur the wrath of any group known for "hanging people by their intestines" (Naoene). However the operation did eventually catch on and received enough support to become a full fledged op.

When news reached the Zetas that there was a threat to their stranglehold of Mexican politics they used their significant sphere of influence to track down a member of Anonymous located in South America and promptly kidnapped him and issued an Ultimatum. The Zetas claimed that they would not only kill the hostage they had but his family and 10 innocent people for every one name that was released as part of the op. Despite some being opposed Anonymous agreed to these demands and the Anon was promptly found relatively unhurt.

This altercation was a significant moment for Anonymous as it marked the first time that it had attacked a criminal conglomerate. Also it marked a very visible switch from lulz to serious international issues. Between this and Anonymous's role in the Arab Spring people were no longer seeing Anonymous as an aimless group but one with an increasingly easier to define agenda. The response by the Zetas also marks the first time that Anons have been threatened with violence and faced punishment outside of the influence of law. Also this was one of the first major op's that did not have the full support of large strands of Anonymous. Even once the op gained momentum large swaths of members opposed this attack and once the threat was delivered there was another divide as to whether or not to give in or not. Many in Anonymous and a vast majority of the public felt that the right thing to do for Mexico would be to release the information and hope that it would clean out the government. If there was a case of the internet not backing an Anonymous decision then that moment would be right then and the negative PR hurt their reputation.

Following the largely failed #opcartel Anonymous needed a boost going into 2012. Unfortunately for them Hector Monsegur, reputed leader of the infamous LULZSEC was caught by the FBI. Facing imminent jail time in a state penitentiary Monsegur aka "Sabu" turned on the LULZSEC in exchange for leniency. The result as of spring 2012 is that six of what the Federal Bureau of Investigation is calling "the world's top hackers" (Esposito) have been arrested and LULZSEC crippled. The validity of these statements are unable to be verified as Anonymous does not have any set leaders so in theory it would be almost impossible to shut down with only 7 people in custody. However this marks a slightly more ominous note for Anonymous in the future. Numerous posts on 4chan have shown a strong threat of violence for the family of Sabu and in early April the Guardian described Lulzsec as "paralyzed". Time will tell what the actual affect will be for Anonymous as a whole.

The hacker culture is one of seclusion and self protection. With the ire of the world's governments and its police forces drawn onto Anonymous the chances of more and more hackers being caught increases. With many of these people not being the typical "hardened" criminal the opportunity to avoid time in the abuse laden penitentiary seems too good to pass up. The arrest of "Sabu" could be seen as just the tipping of the iceberg as lack of loyalty and true leadership could potentially increase the number of arrests and slowly erode at Anonymous support group and cause it to slowly dissipate.

Works Cited

"Anonymous Swoop on Mexico on Gov't Sites in Copyright Protest." RT (2012) <http://rt.com/news/anonymous-mexico-sopa-acta-941/>.

Barkham, Patrick. "Hackers Declare War on Scientology Amid Claims of Heavy Handed Cruise Control." The Guardian (2008).

"Church of Scientology : Anonymous Will be Stopped." WikiNews (2008).

Crabbe, Lauren. "This is what an Anonymous Protest Looks Like." PC World (2011).

Esposito, Richard and Aaron Katersky and Pierre Thomas. "LulzSec "Leader Turns on Fellow Hactivists : Feds." ABC News (2012).

Flock, Elizabeth. "Anonymous Cancels Operations Aginst Drug Cartel,Says Kidnapped Members have been found." Washington Post (2011).

Ho, Vivian. "Anonymous Planning another BART Protest." The San Francisco Chronicle 8/11/11 2011, sec. The Bay Area and State:.

McMillan, Robert. "Bay Area Transit Police Cut Mobile Service to Thwart Protest." PC World (2011) <http://www.pcworld.com/article/238018/bay_area_transit_police_cut_mobile_service_to_thwart_protest.html?tk=rel_news>.

Morris, Scott. "At Least 45 Arrested in BART Protest Monday Night, another Planned Next Week." SF Appeal 2011, sec. News:.

Naoene, Erica. "Anonymous Won't Expose Mexican Cartels "Servants"." Reuters (2011).

Norton, Quinn. "Anonymous Skeptical of Planned Attack on Zetas." Wired Magazine (2011).

The Ethics of Copyright in the Digital Age

Cory Stumpf

Given the innumerable challenges brought up against contemporary copyright laws, it seems necessary for us to explore the ethical implications of copyright laws and the piracy of copyrighted materials. We live in a world in which we all hold copyrights of some kind, from academic papers to personal works of art, and these works are protected under our legal system. It is an interesting dilemma, because media pirates and proponents of strict copyright laws both often feel a sense of moral righteousness in their actions. Pirates sometimes consider themselves protectors of consumer rights because they feel people shouldn't have to pay exorbitant amounts for software that can be copied endlessly for next to nothing. Those who support strict copyright laws, on the other hand, feel that people are entitled to their own intellectual property. We deserve to hold control of our own creations, and people shouldn't be allowed to take them. It is an interesting ethical dilemma, in which both sides claim a moral high ground. In order to solve this, it seems prudent to examine this conflict through the lens of different schools of philosophical thought, and attempt to make the ethical implications of copyright apparent.

Nearly every ethical theorist agrees that stealing is inherently wrong, for various reasons, but the question becomes: is digital piracy stealing? By conventional definitions of theft, it requires an act of taking of personal property with intent to deprive the rightful owner of it. This is problematic in terms of digital piracy because there is no tangible property that is taken, and also the act doesn't deprive the owner of the work, because once a work is digitalized it can be copied infinitely. The owner isn't deprived of property, but rather of profit. During the 18th century, when copyright was first becoming common, there were two common arguments. First, many claimed that intellectual property can be compared to real estate, and that the right of ownership derives from a right of "occupation." William Blackstone argued in his *Commentaries* (1765-1769) that by publishing a book one is not simply offering something for public use, as when land is given for use as a highway. Rather, "In such a case, it is more like making a way through a man's own private grounds, which he may stop at pleasure; he may give out a number of keys, by publishing a number of copies; but no man who receives a key, has thereby a right to forge others, and sell them to other people."[1]

---

[1] William Blackstone, *Commentaries on the Laws of* England 4 vols. (Oxford, 1765-1769) 2:406.

Thus, Blackstone asserted an analogy between real property and the more abstract intellectual property over which one has a right of occupation. By Blackstone's logic, public access to copyrighted works is not a public right but a kind of visitation right. Copyright infringement is thus not so much theft as trespassing. Although he was talking more about printed materials, this analogy works even better when put into the context of the internet. Websites such as YouTube offer the ability to listen and enjoy, but copying data from that website seems ethically wrong.

The second argument originally used in the 18th century identifies the production of the text with the author himself. The text is uniquely tied to its origin through the personality of the author. It serves as a sort of extension of the author, therefore the expression that is embodied in the printed text is quintessentially personal property. The argument from occupation satisfies a similar intuition in a different way. It harkens back to a notion of original appropriation, essentially saying we have a right to make a claim to previously unclaimed things we discover. Prior to its expression by the author, the work was like unowned property, and through her labor she has brought it into existence.[2] Both of the arguments presented offer compelling accounts on the justification of the protection of intellectual property from the perspective of 18th century thinkers.

Next, we should look at specific philosophical schools of thought. First, Immanuel Kant, influential thinker of the Enlightenment, had some distinct opinions about copyright and intellectual property Kant writes in section 31/II of the *Metaphysics of Morals*: "Why does unauthorized publishing, which strikes one even at first glance as unjust, still have an appearance of being rightful? Because on the one hand a book is a corporeal artifact (opus mechanicum) that can be reproduced (by someone in legitimate possession of a copy of it), so that there is a right to a thing with regard to it. On the other hand a book is also a mere discourse of the publisher to the public, which the publisher may not repeat publicly without having a mandate from the author to do so (praestatio operae), and this is a right against a person. The error consists in mistaking one of these rights for the other"[3] Kant seems to support the claim that an author (or artist, musician, etc. when applied contemporarily) has an inherent right to his creation, and thus he would probably support the existence of copyright laws.

In regard to piracy, the Kantian perspective seems to value the concept of ownership a lot more than fair pricing for the consumer. As Kant says in Of the Illegitimacy of Pirate Publishing "The copy that the publisher has had printed is a work of the author (opus) and belongs entirely to the publisher, once he has negotiated for the manuscript or a printed copy, so that he can do whatever he wants with it that can be done in his own name; for that is requisite to a full right

---

[2] Alfino, Mark "Intellectual Property and Copyright Ethics," Business and Professional Ethics Journal, 10.2 (1991): 85-109. Reprinted in Robert A. Larmer (Ed.), Ethics in the Workplace, Minneapolis, MN: West Publishing Company, 1996, 278-293.

[3] Kant, Immanuel *Metaphysics of Morals* 1902, Cambridge University Press, Apr 18, 1996 t.8, p.84

to a thing, that is, to a property. But such use as he can make of it only in the name of another (namely of the author) is an affair (opera) that this other carries on through the owner of the copy, and for this a separate contract is required, besides the one in regard to property"[4] It seems clear that from a Kantian perspective the right to a work belongs solely to its creator, and it seems innately wrong to acquire another's work without compensation.

From a strictly utilitarian perspective, copyright and piracy are a very different issue. A utilitarian analysis requires us to determine what would produce the greatest good for the greatest number, in other words, what will produce the most pleasure in the absence of pain. The obvious first reaction would be to say copyright shouldn't exist, and there should be a free exchange of information in which all could share in every production. In essence, this would legalize piracy. This could, however, be problematic. There is no doubt that, financially, this benefits a greater number of people, while having obvious detrimental effect on some, but the problem becomes a matter of motivation. If there is no profit incentive, it doesn't seem hard to imagine that people will not work as hard to produce great things. It should be noted, however, that there are many systems that are set up that way, for the common good, that function just fine. For instance, Wikipedia contributors aren't seeking a profit, but rather they wish to share their knowledge for the common good. It is difficult to say whether or not legalizing piracy would create more happiness or not because it requires an extremely intricate analysis of the pros and cons of both sides, but it seems that, overall, copyright laws produce less pleasure than if they weren't to exist at all.[5]

Another philosopher who had very influential perspectives on the concept of property is John Locke. Locke's labor theory of property states that property originally comes about by the exertion of labor upon natural resources. Following the argument the fruits of one's labor are one's own because one worked for it. Furthermore the laborer must also hold a natural property right in the resource itself because - as Locke believes - exclusive ownership was immediately necessary for production. To put this into different terms, humans obtain property through their labor, so any "property" we have that isn't the fruit of our own labor isn't actually ours. This only seems to apply, however, to tangible property, rather than an intangible idea in the realm of noumena. Locke himself didn't actually try to justify intangible property. He appears, in fact, to have viewed copyright as merely a policy tool for promoting the public good. More pointedly, copyright actually contradicts Locke's original justification of property. He described legislation that authorized the Stationers' Company monopoly on printing, which was the nearest thing to actual copyright in his day, as a "manifest . . . invasion of the trade, liberty, and property of the subject." Even in the present day, copyright holder can impose prior restraint, fines, imprisonment, and confiscation on those engaged in peaceful expression and the

---

[4] Kant *Metaphysics of Morals* 1902, Cambridge University Press, Apr 18, 1996 t.8, p.84

[5] Harper, Jim *Getting Intellectual About Property* The Technology Liberation Front , February, 14, 2006 http://techliberation.com/2006/02/14/gettin-intellectual-about-property/

quiet enjoyment of physical property by invoking the power of the government. As one author put it, "By thus gagging our voices, tying our hands, and demolishing our presses, copyright law violates the very rights that Locke defended."[6] The main point is that far too often people mistake the fact that Locke posited that we have a natural right to property derived from our labor to mean that we have a right to receive compensation for all uses and derivations of our labor, which is a bit fallacious.

An important distinction Locke makes is the concept of "fencing" of property. Taken literally with real property, fencing makes trespassing difficult, but, more importantly to Locke, the concept of fencing also includes giving notice to others that the property has an owner. This is significant in terms of society; if one was to walk up to a fallow field or an apple tree, how would he know if it was already owned if it were unfenced? Intellectual property is, unfortunately, very difficult to fence, because it isn't easy to trace the origin of every idea. One somewhat alarming example is the fact that even those who discover a gene can get a patent on that particular genetic sequence. This means that researchers who want to use a gene need to pay the patent holder in order to conduct research. In other words, the product of one person's labor is inhibiting the labor of another, and Locke would undoubtedly disagree with this.

Obviously there are many ethical implications that come with the existence of copyright, and there is no concrete moral answer. It seems clear that people do deserve some natural right to the things that they produce, but the main question is whether or not all things derived from that idea deserve protection under copyright as well. Should we be able to copyright ideas? This seems like a slippery slope, and could quite possibly limit our creativity and enjoyment of information and media. Those advocating for a completely free exchange of information, software, and media generally are doing what they feel is morally right, but it seems necessary to offer at least some protection to the intellectual property of individuals. It is an interesting dilemma; legislators will be faced with many ethical challenges in the coming years, and thus will have to rely on the wisdom presented by philosophers such as these to make their decisions.

Works Cited

---

[6] Bell, Tom M. *Locke on Copyright* The Technology Liberation Front , December 20, 2007 http://techliberation.com/2007/12/20/locke-on-copyright/

Alfino, Mark "Intellectual Property and Copyright Ethics," Business and Professional Ethics Journal, 10.2 (1991): 85-109. Reprinted in Robert A. Larmer (Ed.), Ethics in the Workplace, Minneapolis, MN: West Publishing Company, 1996, 278-293.

Blackstone, William *Commentaries on the Laws of* England 4 vols. (Oxford, 1765-1769) 2:406.

Bell, Tom M. *Locke on Copyright* The Technology Liberation Front , December 20, 2007 http://techliberation.com/2007/12/20/locke-on-copyright/

Kant, Immanuel *Metaphysics of Morals* 1902, Cambridge University Press, Apr 18, 1996 t.8, p.84

Harper, Jim *Getting Intellectual About Property* The Technology Liberation Front , February, 14, 2006 http://techliberation.com/2006/02/14/gettin-intellectual-about-property/

Copyright and The Music Industry

Ryan Thompson

Advancements in modern technology, most notable the MP3, have caused the music industry to call for an increase in regulation of copyright laws. The music industry claims to have lost significant amounts of revenue due to piracy and other methods of copyright infringement such as bootlegging. The music industry believes these violations pose a significant economic threat to the record industry including the artists. A study done by the Institute for Policy Innovation, sited by the Recording Industry Association of America, states that piracy causes an: "Annual harm at $12.5 billion dollars in losses to the US economy."[1] As technology advances and copyright laws become more prevalently questioned, the music industry needs to advance it's marketing to better economically encompass the ever-popular idea of free music access through the Internet. The music industry faces a wide variety of difficulties in enforcing copyright laws that are both costly and ineffective. Although piracy poses detrimental revenue loss, it is not the only copyright issue the US record industry faces. Termination rights also pose a significant threat to the music industry. First piracy will be explored in its various forms and what geographical limitations the government has in enforcing those laws. Then, termination rights and the battle between copyright holders and artists will be discussed and the threats it posses to the industry.

Copyright enforcement faces a variety of constraints, one primary obstacle is the geographical restraints they face when pursuing pirating sites. Often pirating sites are based out of countries that do not enforce copyright laws. Copyright holders face financial burdens by trying to pursue file-sharing websites located in countries that protect them under law. In 2005, prosecutors determined the Russian site AllofMP3.com was not in violation of state law because Russian copyright laws only pertained to physical property such as CDs, not MP3s[2]. This costly pursuit of copyright law hurts the music industry in two ways. First, most obviously, the media industry has to pay the legal costs of these unsuccessful trials and pursuits. The second, being far more financially

---

[1] http://www.riaa.com/physicalpiracy.php?content_selector=piracy_details_online

[2] http://www.emle.org/_data/Volker_Lehmann__Copyright_in_the_Music_Industry.pdf

detrimental, is the fact that these cases send the message to pirating sites around the world that they can legally function in countries without copyright laws. Unfortunately in terms of piracy, file sharing sites are not the only foreign market that violates US copyright law.

The reproduction and sale of unauthorized copies has become a prevalent problem for US copyright holders. These counterfeit reproductions are sold on the streets and in market places all over the world. CD burning equipment has become increasingly cheap to purchase and operate, making bootleg CDs a legitimate source of lossed revenue for the record industry. The RIAA stated this about street piracy: "legitimate sales are being replaced by sales of counterfeit goods, and the people who create, package and legally sell music are paying the price. The damage is real and demonstrable and undercuts the economic foundation of the most creative and vibrant music industry in the world."[3]

Article 1, Section 8, Clause 8 of the United States Constitution empowers congress to: "To promote the Progress of Science and useful Arts, by securing for limited Times to Authors and Inventors the exclusive Right to their respective Writings and Discoveries."[4] Granting free access to music does not hinder the artist's financial ability to further the progression of his or her craft. By eliminating the high costs of major labels (recording, distribution, creating the actual CD, promotion, and marketing) artists can actually increase profits by creating free access to music.

With the advancements in modern technology, it has become increasing cheaper to purchase recording equipment. More and more self-recordings and even small labels are cutting the costs of recording significantly, making it more cost effective to avoid major labels. Artists can also drastically reduce the costs of distribution and promotion by uploading their music to file sharing sites. This is far more efficient than traditional forms of distribution because an artist simply has to upload a track costly little to no money and he or she instantly gains a worldwide audience. In many respects the audience is vastly greater through Internet distribution as it can reach anywhere in the world. This also cuts away the marketing price as the artist's reputation spreads much more significantly and rapidly. Where artist's profit by distributing they're music for free is with an increased worldwide audience and the positive externalities from avoiding major labels. This increased worldwide audience leads to a greater profit from live performances. The Internet distribution also can lead to developing audiences in other parts of the world, creating a foreign market. Unfortunately for the record industry piracy is not the only predicament they face.

The Copyright Law of 1976 has a provision in it stating that artists can seek to reclaim their recordings after thirty-five years. A lobbyist for the record industry stated that termination rights are: "a life threatening change for them, the legal equivalent of Internet technology."[5] The provision is only applicable to

---

[3] http://www.riaa.com/physicalpiracy.php?content_selector=piracy_details_street

[4] http://www.usconstitution.net/const.html#A1Sec8

artists that file for termination two years in advance. This makes January 1st, 2013 the first date artists can reclaim their work due to the fact that the Copyright Law of 1976 went into affect in 1978. This provision has polarized artists and major record labels and will undoubtabely result in a legal battle likely to reach the Supreme Court.

Due to the loss of revenue from piracy the record industry has become "disproportionately dependant on sales of older recordings in their catalogs."[6] But the record labels plan on legally battling artists on the grounds that termination rights do not apply. The record industry is taking a stance that artists are "works for hire"[7] or essentially an employee of the record industry, which would trounce termination rights. However, the legal representatives of artists seeking termination disagree with the notion that artists are employees for a variety of reasons. One prominent argument is that artists typically pay for their own recordings through deductions in future royalties. Also, another significant argument is that artists are not employees because they do not receive employee benefits. A copyright expert from Columbia University School of Law sums up this argument by stating: "Where do they work? Do you pay Social Security for them? Do you withdraw taxes from a paycheck? Under those kinds of definitions it seems pretty clear that your standard recording artist…is not an employee but an independent contractor."[8] This argument will likely be decided in court, setting a new legal precedent for termination rights. But there is also an independent argument that termination rights could actually hurt the artist economically in the long run.

If termination rights are granted to artists, the result for the record labels will be a significant economic loss. It is also important to recognize that termination rights only affect a small minority of artists that have reached a popularity where reclaiming their work would see significant returns in revenue. If artists are granted the right to reclaim their work it will result in a significant loss in revenue for the record labels. This is turn will hurt artists negotiating new deals because the labels will have less to offer to make up for their potential loss of revenue. So termination rights could have a result that "forces initial prices down for all artists. It then enriches a few fortunate enough to have produced works of enduring value A termination provision, in other words, is like a lottery ticket—and like lottery tickets, the vast majority of ticket holders get nothing."[9] Essentially termination rights only aid the artists who need it the least, while hurting other artists. Many prominent artists such as Bob Dylan, Bill Joel, and

---

[5] http://www.nytimes.com/2011/08/16/arts/music/springsteen-and-others-soon-eligible-to-recover-song-rights.html?pagewanted=all

[6] http://www.nytimes.com/2011/08/16/arts/music/springsteen-and-others-soon-eligible-to-recover-song-rights.html?pagewanted=all

[7] http://www.copyright.gov/circs/circ09.pdf

[8] http://www.law.columbia.edu/faculty/faculty_news/2011/August2011

[9] http://www.freakonomics.com/2011/08/31/the-music-industry-copyright-battle-when-is-owning-more-like-renting/

Bruce Springsteen have filed for termination and how the courts favor in these cases will likely become the legal standard for future artists and record labels.

It has become increasingly evident that the current business model adopted by major record labels is failing. By eliminating costly pursuits trying to expel copyright violations, the record industry could save money best suited for advancing technologically. This advancement could open up new streams of revenue for both the artists and major labels. Furthermore if artists chose to release music independently and without cost it would greatly advance their popularity thus making the artist more revenue. The current copyright laws being upheld by the record industries simply are not working. The rulings from the January 1st, 2013 termination rights legal battles may increasingly cause record labels to adjust their business model. Significant losses of revenue will force them to either adapt or cease to exist.

Copyright and U.S. Relations

Benjamin Tibbs

Copyright has been able to allow singers, actors, movie studio production companies, authors, record label companies and many other individuals and related industries to have control over the pieces of work that they have created. These art forms are also known as forms of Intellectual Property. Those people who go to a movie theater, buy a CD, rent a movie, buy a book or pay to download these art forms are paying for the privilege to share the experience of these works. Since entering the current digital age, copyright infringement here at home is out of control. Internationally copying has become almost unenforceable beyond the boundaries of the United States. In the following pages I am going to discuss the Intellectual wars that have developed with regards to copyright here at home, talk about business dilemmas, and solutions for moving forward as a country.

The free flow of information in today's high-tech world has become a major flash point between those who create works of art by putting their energies into movie production with feature films, printing production with books, audio production with music sound-bites on CDs or similar forms of recordable devices, and those who believe that with the ease of use in the cyber world to copy such materials, these works of art should be free to copy and share. Part of the argument is that we as a nation have just technologically outgrown the confines of older generational periods. The eighteenth century is long gone and the country needs to change with the times, adapting to advances of present reality. In his book The Patent Wars, Fred Warshofsky quoted Pamela Samuelson, who teaches law in Pittsburgh, saying:

> The drafters of the Constitution, educated in the Enlightenment tradition, shared that era's legacy of faith in the enabling powers of knowledge for society as well as the individual. Our current copyright laws, which protect the expression of information, but not the information itself, are based on the belief that unfettered and widespread dissemination of information promotes technological progress (similarly for patent laws which protect devices and processes, not the information about them).' Samuelson further questioned whether in entering the Information Age, where information is the source of greatest wealth, we have outgrown the Enlightenment tradition and are coming to treat information as property. (Warshofsky 1994, p. 177)

Information and the ease of its use on the Internet certainly have made the ability to view it instantaneous, and in many cases free. It is exactly this fact that has made the art industries cringe and do everything they can to stop this from happening. But many say it can't be stopped. Pirates don't see these industries as viable any longer. Many pirates believe that the internet will take away the value of this intellectual property. Paul Paradise points this out in, *Trademark, Counterfeiting, Product Piracy, And The Billion Dollar Threat To The U.S. Economy*: "Many of the pirates operate under a philosophy whose underlying proposition is that the Internet will erode and ultimately transform the value of intellectual property." (Paradise 1999, p. 233)

The Pirate party is one organization that has recently come to existence which supports the abolishment of such things as patent law, and also to reform copyright law. Patent law according to them needs to be abolished to save lives citing pharmaceutical companies and their monopolies over such important research. As for copyright, the Pirate party believes that it should be reformed to regain a lost balance that promoted the spread of culture. If it is not being used commercially it should be free according to them. (www.piratpartiet.se) Of course the Pirate party hasn't been the only ones to reject the idea of copyright law. In fact the battle is more than a century old. "In 1842 the concept of an international copyright was still quite new...Most European countries had not yet become signatories...No matter how much morality might suggest that literary piracy was simple robbery, Americans were deeply suspicious about international copyright." (Simmons 2000, p. 109) This was in relation to American press and the pirating of Charles Dickens' works. Dickens had met notable men of their day and tried to bring some influence to bear on the government's handling of copyright law. He met with Henry Clay, who had been trying for years to gain recognition for international copyright law.

Another notable person who had rallied against copyright law was Henry Carey. Carey "...played a leading role in the formation of the Republican party..." and "...paved the way for the nomination of Lincoln..." Carey believed that a copyright treaty with Britain at the time was not constitutional since it was only ratified through the Senate, and that internationalization of Intellectual ideas was not a right. (Johns 2009, p. 309-311) Many saw this advance of copyright as intrusive to the intellectual freedom of Americans.

There is another side that disagrees with the decentralization of information and its free flow amongst people. They argue that intellectual ideas are actually property since they created the idea any profit that comes from their creation is illegal, pirated and some kind of counterfeit. First, what is intellectual property? According to Warshofsky, and most of the world, intellectual property has two categories: one is industrial and the other is arts. "Artistic works are literary, musical, photographic, cinematographic, paintings, drawings, jewelry and furniture designs, choreography, records, tapes, broadcasts, and the like." (Warshofsky p. 7) These art works are protected by copyright, while many other forms of creation or ideas are protected with patent or trademark laws.

Of course who better to back up anyone in the United States than some of our very own founders? "The patent system represents the vision of America's founding fathers of rewarding innovation for society's greater good. Article 1, Section 8 of the Constitution of the United States provides that 'Congress shall have power...To promote the progress of science and useful Arts, by securing for limited times to authors and Inventors the exclusive right to their perspective Writings and discoveries.'" (Warshofsky p. 31) In the passed copyright act of 1976 permission was given for creators to "(1) reproduce their works, (2) distribute the reproductions, (3) display and perform the work publicly, (4) prepare derivative works, and (5) authorize others to do these things." (Paradise p. 9) There were many criteria for actually being able to put a copyright onto a piece of work. So in order for innovation to thrive and be able to allow a creator the latitude for success, his works of art, at least for a time period, were to be protected.

The video and music record companies are perhaps some of the most vulnerable businesses in the artistic enterprises today. Their forms of distribution include DVDs, CDs, and similar merchandise which are small and are user friendly; unfortunately they are also easy to copy. "Piracy in the entertainment industries is largely a problem of unauthorized copying. Much of the technology is readily available and sold without restriction. Not only are the products easy to duplicate, but much of the success of the entertainment industry rests on a handful of big-name artists. Most counterfeiting in the music industry involves analog cassettes and compact discs (CDs); in the motion picture industry, video cassettes." (Paradise p. 35) Since his book was written many things have changed in the transitioning world of technology. CDs are the mainstay of music recording and the cassette tapes and players are ancient history now; the same is true for video cassette tapes which have been replaced by DVDs. But these forms too are soon becoming obsolete as technology moves faster and faster with time.

There are of course movements to stop piracy even as it becomes less likely to do much good in stopping it, and there are five key piracy areas that involve the art industry which are being focused on: book piracy, film and video piracy, signal theft, video game piracy, and music piracy. Book piracy is the oldest form and was right in the middle of early copyright law development. Eventually forms of protection were formed for the owners of their literary works, England being one of the first. After the French revolution and chaos from free printing and copying that followed in 1789, France too established a copyright law. Of course the United States had copyright law but only for its own citizens and many of the developed countries of the time were in the same position that the United States finds itself in with regard to pirate heavy markets in places like Asia. "In 1996, the IIPA estimated that U.S. Copyright industries lost $10.8 billion due to piracy in fifty-five countries. This was a conservative estimate based on seventy-one countries." (Paradise p. 132)

Film and video pirating is mainly due to the advent of the VCR. In the United States "...5 to 15 percent of all videos rented are counterfeit...in many countries...100 percent, effectively shutting out U.S. Distributors." (Paradise p. 135) Before the VCR, piracy of motion pictures was relatively minor. But it is the ease of recording that made the VCR so dangerous to the film and production industries. As VCRs became readily available, counterfeiting VCRs and cassettes became almost impossible to stop outside of the United States. Inside the United States however, the Film and Video Security Office conducted raids on illegal operations and "...became one of the most successful anti piracy operations in the world...A majority of the 2,644 lawsuits filed in 1988 involved criminal action." (Paradise p. 144)

Signal Theft is another form of piracy involving the successful tapping of signal wave frequencies. According to Paradise there are two kinds of signal theft: satellite and cable. Satellite involves intercepting programmer's transmission signals, and cable involves a descrambling device hooked up to a TV to clear the picture. In 1984 the Cable Communications Policy Act of 1984 made signal theft a federal crime.

Pirated video games also became a problem. In the 1980s, arcade games became the craze and with its rising popularity piracy also rose. One of the major problems was counterfeit circuit boards being used in the arcade games. What made arcade games unusually hard to find was the fact that it was another form of computer piracy and the diversity to which arcade games are found made it difficult to prosecute cases. The result has been enforcement being held only at the customs level.

Finally, music piracy has accounted for "...$300 million sales in 1997. The worldwide loss figure for music piracy in 1995 was estimated at $5 billion..." (Paradise p. 159) Music was a little late to the copyright game and came into the fold in 1976 when the Copyright Act guaranteed protection of sound recordings. In the music industry "Piracy in the primary market was practically eliminated after several executives of the Sam Goody chain were indicted for the interstate transportation and sale of counterfeit sound recordings." (Paradise p. 163)

Many of the piracy crime continue today. The main problem area that the United States has had is outside of the country's borders. Within the borders the United States has been able to curtail piracy and keep it relatively low. However with advancing technology and more ways to pirate book, video, signal, gaming, and music industries it is going to be an ongoing problem unless the government and corporations can keep up with these advances.

The struggle that not many people pay attention to and indeed may have little sympathy for is the costs that goes into making the productions that so many of us love. Whether it's our favorite movies or our favorite songs, one thing pirating does do is inflict considerable loss on the investment made by these companies. How many people think about the kinds of investments that go into a film production? I would say not many, but the fact is that it takes millions of investment dollars to produce a movie and the amount earned back doesn't even begin to pay off until at least two years after the film's release depending on how much those production costs were. Copyright helps to keep those who would copy from stealing, because that is just what it is, stealing. The amount that goes into making a movie is quite substantial. "And in fact a typical Hollywood movie costs $25 to $30 million to put in the can. Another $20 to $30 million is spent for distribution, advertising, and other expenses. 'by the time you're done,' points out

Lang, 'you've got a game in which you can't play unless you've got or can control $50 million.'" (Warshofsky p. 265-6)

In the international arena there are more details to worry about and piracy becomes a serious issue when U.S. Law can't do anything to prosecute violations. Basically it is up to the business and how much risk it wants to take along with the government protecting business here at home. So with that there are three things that will ultimately help U.S. Businesses overseas; businesses must choose their markets wisely, both businesses and the government must evolve in order to survive and the government must work on copyright solutions in order to keep its intellectual property innovators on top.

In order for a business to survive, it needs to make sure that it is getting involved with a market whose protections are much like that of the United States. The example that shows why businesses don't get involved with some markets is portrayed in Jack Goldsmith and Tim Wu's book, *Who Controls The Internet*, with Russia being an example. Russia's "...economy is the tenth largest in the world...Nonetheless, multinational Internet companies like eBay do not provide services there. At first glance this is a puzzle...But Russia has the opposite problem. It suffers from private harms gone unchecked: insecurity of private property, corporate fraud, a failed criminal law system, organized crime and oligarch-dominated business, and ineffective respect for and enforcement of contract rights." (Goldsmith & Wu 2006, p. 144-5) The lesson here is for businesses to choose countries that show regulatory respect for businesses and intellectual property. Similar copyright law is one area that should be considered when entering that countries market.

Secondly, both the government and the businesses seeking new markets must be able, willing and actively seeking innovated ways to stay ahead of the technological curve, finding ways to beat infringement, cyber pirating and "Free Riding." What is free riding? Free riding is a term used to describe countries that pirate another country's valuable research and make knock off copies in order to make a profit. Many of these free riders aren't using innovation of their own, however these knock off business sectors are major parts of some countries who are struggling as third world or second world component countries. Some countries that free ride are Brazil, Mexico, Thailand and many other parts of Asia, and Southeast Asia. These are just a few, there are many more around the globe.

New technology can help to fight against piracy. "In 1993 the Clinton administration proposed a new standard for encryption technology developed with the National Security Agency. The Technology was known as the Clipper Chip, because it used a secret algorithm called Skipjack to encrypt information. The Clipper Chip was considered impossible to crack..." (Paradise p. 244) The Clipper Chip failed because the American public was skeptical about the anti-privacy measure within it that seemed to leave an open door for police to invade personal space. This measure was called "LEAF" or law enforcement access field.

Recently the SIPA/SOPA acts were proposed in order to bolster copyright infringement crackdown but it has been unpopular with the public as well. The point to both of these though is that the industry is trying to keep intellectual property relevant, and the government, though unsuccessful, recently is thinking outside of the box and this is a healthy sign that may result in positive handling of all the illegal piracy going on. But this is on the domestic front; we need some laws that protect us from the little countries that are stealing our ideas, possible trade laws or sanctions to level the playing field.

Third is the government must work on intellectual property rights on an international basis. Some places that may be looked upon to help with overall enforcement of intellectual property rights are places such as the UN and the EU. The United States could pursue more treaties with countries in order to work closer together on stopping piracy and fraud. The United States could make use of its Trade and Tariff laws, and heavily pursue a domestic program that would not alienate the public but enforce piracy and intellectual property laws and make a few examples in order to curb abuse. Some remedies include heavy fines, which already exist, moving some computer crimes to more than just misdemeanor, and continue an aggressive policy in support of sting operations in order to show everyone that it is not a joke to break the law through pirating or any other intellectual property theft. Working with other law enforcement groups, and government agencies would also prove to be helpful and productive.

In conclusion I have gone over some of the struggles with intellectual property and some different views for and against copyright. I have gone over the business perspective and some of the financial troubles and fraud that burden them. And I have mentioned the importance of the government's critical role in the arena of copyright and the importance of continual involvement with enforcement of would be law breakers. In the end perhaps the digital world is moving so fast that our methods are outdated and are only meant for a conventional world.

Kopimism: A New Religion

Emma Wabunsee-Kelly

Religion has played an influential role in every aspect of society and social order from the beginning of time. Religion has served as the basis for culture and community structure due to the moralistic implications and outward practice of various religions. In more recent times, social order has separated from its link to religion while individuals and countries alike are establishing new ideas of moral and correct behavior. A new social order in our very own modern times has stemmed from a technological revolution. The internet has facilitated communication and the spread of information in a way that has influenced multiple social and cultural revolutions. The Middle East in particular has taken advantage of the internet in recent times to spread information and gather both political and social support. Other parts of the world, the United States and Europe as well, have utilized the internet as a primary means of education and awareness surrounding social and cultural issues. However, religion has developed due to the influence of culture and independent ideals so that religions now allow individuals to express worship and praise to a variety of different beings. The world's newest established religion, Kopimism, aims to support the free spread of information via internet to all individuals throughout the globe by supporting pirate ideologies and by actively establishing a system of belief and practice surrounding the sharing of information.

The Missionary Church of Kopimism was founded in Sweden in 2010 and is protected under the freedom of religion as given by the Constitution of Sweden (Gale Group). The Church's founder, Isak Gerson, attempted to establish the Church as an official religion three times before the claim was accepted. The third and last attempt to found the Church took over a year to be approved by the Swedish government (George). The Swedish constitution aims to protect all religions' right to practice and to protect one's religious freedom. The constitution also protects against legal and private discrimination surrounding religion and religious persons (International Religious Freedom Report). Sweden as a country officially recognizes the Church of Sweden as the official religious institution; however, only one in ten Swedes recognizes religion and ritual as a factor in daily activities (Celsing). Sweden proves to be a culturally diverse country ideal to host a new age religion due to the protection from the country's government and the support of the country's population.

The Missionary Church of Kopimism exists as Sweden's and the world's newest and most groundbreaking religion. The Church founded its name around the root word "kopimi" which translates to "copy me." A Kopimist is a person with the philosophical belief that all information should be freely shared, distributed, and unrestricted. Not only do Kopimists share information among each other, but the group actively attempts to spread information throughout the public sector through individual action and by supporting other groups that hold the same or similar ideals. Kopimism opposes copyright law and supports piracy by groups such as The Pirate Bay and the spread of information from organizations like Wikileaks.

The Missionary Church of Kopimism's founder, Isak Gerson, is a 19 year old philosophy student at Uppsala University in Sweden. Gerson's finesse for philosophy and technology gave him a definite foundation for the formation of the Church; however, Gerson was not alone in his desire to found a Church surrounding his philosophical belief that information should be freely spread. Peter Sunde, a founding member of The Pirate Bay, originally had the idea to establish Kopimism as an official Swedish religion but never followed through. Sunde and Gerson both were inspired by Ibi "Kopimi" Botani, a founding member of The Pirate Bay, who passed away unexpectedly in 2010. Gerson's initiative finally payed off in 2010 when the Church was accepted by the Swedish government and established as a finite institution (Rollo).

Kopimists specifically abide by the Constitution of Kopimism, which is a document that has been translated into multiple different languages and depicts the rules, regulations, and responsibilities members of the Church are encouraged to abide by. There are six foundations that Kopimists abide by: copying of information is ethically right, dissemination of information is ethically right, copy-mixing is a type of sacred copying, copying or remixing information communicated by another person is seen as an act of respect and a strong expression of acceptance and Kopimistic faith, the internet is holy, and code is law. The Church appoints operators that dedicate their lives to the Kopimist faith, and to encourage other members to do the same. Operators effectively dedicate their lives to copying and remixing information in the name of Kopimism. The Constitution goes on to explain sacred symbols, digital services, the community, and other values and responsibilities held within the Church (First United Church Of Kopimism, US).

Kopimism has often been question by Christianity and critics alike. Kopimists have often been referred to as a cult; however, the Missionary Church of Kopimism has a firm set of basic moral beliefs. While Kopimists do not necessarily believe in one central God, members of the Church worship the act of copying and sharing information. Much like Christians who worship the Bible and other sacred figures and symbols, Kopimists have sacred practices and symbols as well. Control+C and Control+V would be comparable to an image of Mary, and the signature "K" symbol for Kopimism is just as significant as a cross. Much like other religions, Kopimists practice religion through service as well. With the aid of technological innovation Kopimists all over the world meet in online chat rooms with the intent to partake in Kopyactings, or the share of information through copy and remix among each other. Kopimists view their acts of sharing not only as worship but the members of the Church call Kopyactings sacrament.

Kopimism's basic practices are much like those of any other church. Kopimists meet and share information together to strengthen the beliefs and relationships among each other. The free flow of information is a basic human right in the eyes of Kopimists, meaning every individual, even those not involved in the Church, have a right to knowledge and understanding of the world around them. The value of information is not only inherently valuable, but information increases in value the more times it is copied and shared or distributed among others. Kopimists not only see sharing information as an individual duty, but the follows of the church recognize the uninhibited distribution of information as a sacrament and something that should be appreciated by all humans.

In relation to Christianity, Kopimism does not necessarily have a final set of moral practices other than to share information among each other; however, Kopimism does offer an interesting and relatable perspective on the afterlife. According to Isak Gerson, Kopimists understand the afterlife in terms of the copying of information as a way to achieve eternal life. The more times a piece of information is copied and shared the better chance that piece of information has of being remembered and significant in the future. Humans do not necessarily have an intrinsic value, only the act of copying has ultimate eternal value. To make better sense of this, compare a Kopimist's afterlife to a Christian's afterlife; in a sense, Kopimism seemingly denies humanity any individual intrinsic value and places value away from the individual and onto data and other intangible materials. While Christianity focuses morality on human action and behavior in combination with loyalty and an acceptance of God.

Another difference or aspect of comparison between Kopimism and Christianity is the difference between censorship in the Christian Church and free range knowledge. Christianity has a long history of deception surrounding the actions of priests and other authoritative figures. Also many critics and believers alike question the legitimacy and truthfulness in the actions and stories explained in the Bible and preached in Church services. Kopimism, although an extremely new religion, fully supports the spread of information and condemns those who act to keep information private or who withhold information from anybody, especially the public. Kopimism is based on a system that honors the individual's right to choose knowledge and awareness above one individual's right to choose for a group of people. Kopimism is democratic in a sense while Christianity has so far proven to be greatly autocratic.

Although Kopimism is a registered religion, there are still many legal ramifications the participants must abide by in order abstain a legal persona. While Kopimism is legally established and therefore protected under the Swedish constitution's freedom of religion, the followers still advocated the sharing of information, which often times violates national and international copyright laws. While the Church does not outright encourage illegal file sharing, the Missionary Church of Kopimism is openly against laws that restrict the sharing of information. The US division of Kopimism has chosen not to respond to the proposed SOPA and ACTA bills, other than to encourage followers of the religion and ideology to install a software program called Tor. "Tor has proven particularly useful in opening up internet-based lines of communication in countries where governments actively censor free speech between individuals and the outside world." (adVATAR). "[Tor] encourages [people and Kopimists alike] to use the internet for creative and life-improving purposes" (adVATAR). Kopimists simply use and encourage other users of the internet to seek self and worldly betterment through the use of online information sources.

Kopimists face multiple social ramifications due to the unknown precedents of the religion. Many Kopimists do not openly practice or inform their families and social circles of their lifestyle choice. Many onlookers view Kopimism as a joke, or illegitimate. However, it is my belief that by sharing the information surrounding Kopimism and the definitive beliefs and practices would enlighten other individuals as well. The public would be more inclined to accept Kopimism and possibly even become believers themselves if they knew the philosophical and moral principles behind the Church's manifesto. The Church is also commonly viewed as a group of young men solely interested in computer programming and software hacking; technicalities that the public is not familiar with. The greatest appeal to the Church, in my opinion is the fact that there is no required induction or membership. Anybody can be a self proclaimed Kopimist, and one must only go to the website and sign up if one should want to officially proclaim membership. Believing in the principles of free information is all it takes to be a Kopimist, therefore I feel there are many more individuals throughout the globe who are only unaware of this new social phenomenon.

Religion is viewed through different cultural and social lenses alike. Kopimism offers a new perspective to view current political and social issues around the world while still relating to a higher philosophical belief. However, there is an underlying rebellious theme to the religion, as the members and founders alike refer to copyright law in a "tongue in cheek" manner. While the spread of information does not always have positive effects, Kopimists only want to better the lives of every individual the members encounter. The beauty of human life and free will is that we can choose to seek out information or to remain in a state of unknowing. Kopimtists only aim to target the human ability to choose education and knowledge. As humans we continually develop and change due to a gain in knowledge and practice. Kopimism combines knowledge and practice into a philosophical belief and a lifestyle that benefits those who choose to partake.

Works Cited:

Celsing, Charlotte. "Are Swedes Losing Their Religion?" Sweden.se, 1 Sept. 2006. Web. 20 Mar. 2012.

"First United Church Of Kopimism", US. Blog at WordPress.com. Web. 24 Mar. 2012.

George, Allison. "Kopimism: The World's Newest Religion Explained." Newscientist.com. New Scientist, 6 Jan. 2012. Web. Mar 20 2012.

"International Religious Freedom Report 2006 - Sweden". U.S. Department of State - Bureau of Democracy, Human Rights, and Labor. 26 October 2009. Web. 20 Mar. 2012.

Nordfeldth, Mikael. MMN-o Blog. Wordpress. Web. 25 Mar. 2012. "Digital Legacy Or Forking The Person Machine?" MMN-o Blog. Blog.mmn-o.se. 11 Nov. 2012. Web. 25 Mar. 2012.

Rollo, Romig. "The First Church Of Pirate Bay." Thenewyorker.com. The New Yorker, 12 Jan. 2012. Web. 3 Mar. 2012.

"SOCIAL STUDIES." Globe & Mail [Toronto, Canada] 9 Jan. 2012: L7. Gale Opposing Viewpoints In Context. Web. 11 Feb. 2012.

"Uppsala University." Wikipedia. Wikimedia Foundation. 14 Mar. 2012. Web. 20 Mar 2012.

Digitalization and the Limits of Copyright Law

Koby Warren

There are always tensions between different generations of technological innovators. Such tensions appear to manifest themselves in US copyright law as older generations seek to protect their stake from the encroachment of new innovations. This theme has played out through US history. Sheet music authors feared the advent of phonograph inventors, which in turn rued the day that radio broadcasts became popular. Now we find that digitalization is threatening the copyright status quo. Yet, digitalization may represent a more urgent threat than those before. By virtue of its rapid development and evolution, digitalization has stretched our current conceptions of copyright law to their limits. The onset of digitalization in the late twentieth century represents a particular challenge for those currently holding copyrights. In light of this challenge, we find ourselves at a point where we must ask: to what extent can we protect copyrighted material? Perhaps even more important is the normative question: should we even protect it in the first place? An inquiry into the history of US copyright law and the challenges levied by increased digitalization, particularly Internet file sharing, will shed some light on these questions.

Copyright law is an old concept within the United States dating all the way back to our founding era. At its foundation, US copyright law assumes that there are two stake holders: authors *and* consumers.[1] Each of these stakeholders has a claim to certain expectations whenever a copyright is considered. The author needs to have peace of mind that he will be able to make a profit when developing new technologies. Otherwise, he may not write anything. On the other hand, there is a sense in which no innovation is truly original. Public consumers also hold a claim to innovations due to their cultural nature. Thomas Jefferson weighed in on copyright when he stated that ideas are something which "an individual may exclusively posses as long as he keeps it to himself; but the moment it is divulged, it forces itself into the possession of every one."[2] This sentiment appears to have been mirrored by James Madison. When discussing the

---

[1] Jessica Litman. *Digital Copyright* (Amherst: Prometheus, 2001.) p. 15. (Hereafter reffered to as: *Litman*).

[2] Jefferson, Thomas. *The Founder's Constitution.* The University of Chicago Press. 2000. http://press-pubs.uchicago.edu/founders/documents/a1_8_8s12.html.

idea of copyright, Madison clearly hesitates to approve copyright monopolies. He feared that granting individuals monopolies like copyright would potentially "produce more evil than good."[3] Between these two founding fathers, there appears to have been hesitation to grant complete monopolies on copyrightable material. The public also has a claim to ideas.

As written in the US Constitution, copyright law has a particular mission. Under article 1, section 8 of the US Constitution, congress has the power to "promote the progress of science and useful arts, by securing for limited times to authors and Inventors the exclusive right to their respective writings and discoveries."[4] By allowing congress to protect authors for a *limited time*, it would appear as though the Constitution also preserves the notion of author and public stakeholders. It is important to note that congressional power to grant copyrights stems from the progress imperative. Embedded here in the Constitution is congress's mission when granting copyrights – encouraging innovation. This imperative applies to digitalization and the challenges it raises to current US copyright regimes.

It is important to note when discussing digitalization's affect on copyright law that since its inception, the balance between authors and consumers has slowly shifted towards the former. The current copyright law as revised in 1976, represents this movement towards broad rights and narrow exceptions.[5] The law grants very broad rights to copyright owners while providing very narrow "fair use" exceptions. These fair use exceptions list copyright uses that do not automatically infringe the rights of owners. Although, they are not necessarily listed as rights. Rather, some legal scholars refer to them as "privileges."[6] Such a status suggests a de-emphasis of consumers in the copyright stakeholder relationship. Here, the challenge is to examine how advancements in Internet file sharing software have rocked this hegemonic interpretation of copyright law.

All this provides a necessary backdrop for specifically discussing digital technology's affect on copyright law. Starting in 1984, copyright owners began to notice that technological advancements were beginning to threaten their interests. These concerns came to a head in *Sony v. Universal City Studios, Inc.* (1984). Known as the "Betamax decision," this case represents a watershed moment for digital technology's relationship to copyright law. The Motion Picture Association of America (MPAA) sought to end what it saw as an egregious encroachment on their copyright laws. They considered Betamax technology a threat towards their ability to ensure control and protection of their copyrighted works.

---

[3] Madison, James. *Monopolies.*
http://www.constitution.org/jm/18191213_monopolies.htm.

[4] "The Constitution of the United States," Article 1, Section 8, Clause 8.

[5] *Litman.* p. 55.

[6] Zohar Efroni, *Access-Right: The Future of Digital Copyright Law* (Oxford: Oxford University Press, 2011.) p. 156. (Hereafter refered to as: *Efroni*).

Specifically, the Betamax decision revolved around the concept of "time shifting." Time shifting is a term that refers to the act of altering the time at which media is available for consumption. In the Betamax case, Sony's technology allowed consumers to record television for later viewing.[7] Copyright holders considered time shifting an infringing practice. The Betamax decision rejected this reasoning by ruling that time shifting was a legitimate, non-infringing use of technology because it involved private and individual use.[8] This ruling established a way that technologies could not be held liable. If they could prove significant non-infringing uses for their technology, then they could potentially avoid liability.[9] This decision is important because later attempts to enforce copyright laws in the digital realm would have to grapple with the standard of non-infringing uses set by this decision. In addition, the Supreme Court's approval of time shifting has become relevant in determining the legality of another type of shifting called "space shifting." Because space shifting involves altering the medium in which media is stored, peer to peer networks have appealed to this decision to protect the digital MP3 versions of copyright material that exist on their networks.

In addition to the Betamax decision's precedent on non-infringing uses, Justice Stevens pointed out an important fact about copyright law. Justice Stevens stated in his brief that traditionally, copyright has to be changed by congress to address technological advancement.[10] This represents a key point in digital copyright history, as lobbies began seeking anti-circumvention laws to bolster copyright protections in light of technological advancements.[11] However, despite industry attempts to secure anti-circumvention laws, digital technology still posed a significant threat. Copyright holders had to turn to litigation to ensure that digital technologies, especially online peer-to-peer networks, complied with the law.

Napster was one of the first high profile online networks to face copyright holder litigation. In 1999, the Recording Industry Association of America (RIAA) filed a lawsuit against the online company. In their brief, the RIAA asserted that Napster was "similar to a giant online pirate bazaar: users log onto Napster servers and make their previously personal MP3 collections available for download by other Napster users who are logged in at the same time."[12] The crux of the argument was that Napster directly facilitated the infringement of copyright protected works. Napster attempted to prove that they were a legitimate company that allowed users to space shift their media.

---

[7] Matthew Rimmer, *Digital Copyright and the Consumer Revolution: Hands Off My iPod* (Edward Elgar Publishing, 2007.) P. 15. (Herafter reffered to as: *Rimmer*).
[8] *Sony Corp. v. Universal City Studios*. 464 U.S. 417 (U.S. Supreme Court, January 17, 1984).
[9] *Rimmer*. p. 64.

[10] *Ibid*. 63.

[11] *Efroni*. p. 291.

[12] *Rimmer*. p. 93.

Unfortunately for Napster, the court didn't agree. Napster's technology appeared to directly facilitated infringement. As such, Napster represents a digital technology that wasn't well adapted to the intricacies of copyright law. After Napster's loss, other online media networks learned from their mistakes and adapted their technology to make copyright litigation more difficult.[13]

In contrast with Napster, Grokster's online peer-to-peer network posed a greater challenge to copyright holders. Rather than have a centralized server, Grokster had decentralized their network making it more difficult to prove that they were directly facilitating copyright infringement.[14] This innovation stretched the Betamax decision to the point where Justice Souter developed the "inducement" rule for copyright liability. Under this rule, a company can be held secondarily liable if they induce infringement by providing a medium for it.[15] Grokster was found guilty in a decision that seemed to indicate the copyright industry's successful preservation of their rights. However, Grokster was not the last peer-to-peer network to pop up on the Internet. There was still a large market seeking access to file sharing networks. Whereas Grokster lost, other technologies arose that made copyright enforcement even more difficult.

BitTorrent technology is the next stage in online peer-to-peer technology. BitTorrent is a completely decentralized technology that relies on reciprocation to share files. There is no central network, which makes it hard to prove direct infringement. Furthermore, downloads are fragmented between multiple users, which makes infringement more difficult to trace. Whereas previous digital networks have been clearly designed for infringement purposes in some way, BitTorrent networks have extensive non-infringement purposes. Because of this fact, BitTorrent represents a distinct challenge to copyright holders. Computer science expert Edward Felton refers to BitTorrent technology as the "litmus test for the Supreme Court standard for inducement."[16] Pursuant to the Betamax case, there appears to be plenty of room to argue that BitTorrent programs offer legitimate mediums to share information that is privately owned and not necessarily copyrighted.

Perhaps going even further is the recent peer-to-peer network program called "Tribler." Tribler also uses a torrent system that is highly decentralized and based on reciprocation between file sharers. The big difference is, Tribler does not require any kind of external website or torrent tracker. This means that it is completely based on peer networks. There is no website to take down or central server to remove. This makes it a problem for copyright holders for two big reasons. First, there would be difficulties proving that it purely induces infringement. Second, to take it down you would have to shut down the entire Internet.[17] Tribler signifies digital technology at its finest when it comes to

---

[13] *Ibid.* p. 96.

[14] *Ibid.* p. 97.

[15] *Ibid.* p. 99.

[16] *Ibid.* p. 114.

avoiding copyright enforcement. It would appear that even if Tribler lost a lawsuit, there would be no way of actually enforcing any court ruling. This demonstrates a looming problem that digitalization poses to current US copyright laws. Enforcement of these laws can only go so far. Even if US copyright law can contain technologies through legal means, programs like Tribler prove that digitalization can potentially move beyond their ability to control it.

BitTorrent and Tribler are unique because they represent digital technology at its extreme when it comes to avoiding copyright enforcement. They allow tons of people to have access to copyrighted material for free. So many people use it that it is fair to say that the proliferation and legal success of such programs symbolizes a kind of movement back to the consumer side of the copyright stakeholder relationship. As shown above, the evolution of online file-sharing technologies paralleled the development of an ongoing battle against copyright holders. Because these technologies have been able to adapt so quickly, they have been able remain in legal grey areas. In doing so, they have stretched not only current understandings of US copyright law but also the ability of copyright holders to enforce their rights. As mentioned, BitTorrent and especially Tribler make it really difficult to enforce infringement laws.

Attempts to take the battle directly to the people have also proven unsuccessful. By attempting to make examples out of individuals, copyright holders have come across as monstrous corporations looking to bullying people. Because peer-to-peer network usage is so culturally wide spread, it's possible that a growing proportion of the public may view such attempts as draconian measures taken to defend rights that fewer and fewer people seem to respect. Furthermore, the current legal climate makes it easy for copyright owners to file suits against innovators that may potentially infringe on their rights. The constant threat of litigation weighs heavy on the minds of creative inventors.[18] As such, it can be argued that the current copyright status quo actually stunts innovation in a way that violates copyright law's constitutional imperative.

The proliferation of such view points leads to one potential conclusion: public perceptions of copyright law may be moving towards the consumer side of the copyright stakeholder spectrum. Digitalization is stretching current conceptions of copyright law that emphasize author rights while deemphasizing consumer stakeholder claims. Digitalization technology, as we have seen through the evolution of Internet "piracy" software, has been systematically empowering the consumer side of this relationship. Consequently, this questions the legitimacy of whether copyright laws should indeed focus more on copyright owners than consumers. After all, property is both a legal and social construct. Property – and perhaps copyright by extension – must receive public recognition in order to carry any real weight.[19] It would appear that for both practical reasons of enforcement and ideological reasons due to changes in societal attitudes, we

---

[17] Ernesto, *Tribler Makes BitTorrent Impossible to Shut Down* (2012. http://torrentfreak.com/tribler-makes-bittorrent-impossible-to-shut-down-120208/.)
[18] *Rimmer*. p. 297.

[19] *Efroni*. p. 69.

should revisit copyright relationships with a renewed emphasis on the consumer stakeholders. This conclusion considers digital technology's ability to both continually evade copyright enforcement attempts and provide free access to copyrighted material to large groups of people.

Bibliography

Efroni, Zohar. *Access-Right: The Future of Digital Copyright Law.* Oxford: Oxford University Press, 2011.

Ernesto. *Tribler Makes BitTorrent Impossible to Shut Down.* 2012. http://torrentfreak.com/tribler-makes-bittorrent-impossible-to-shut-down-120208/.

Fitzdam, Justin D. "Private Enforcement of the Digital Millenium Copyright Act." *Cornell Law Review* (Cornell) 90 (2005).

Gayer, Amit, and Oz Shy. "Copyright Enforcement in the Digital Era." *CESifo Economic Studies* (Institute for Economic Research), 2005.

Jefferson, Thomas. *The Founder's Constitution.* The University of Chicago Press. 2000. http://press-pubs.uchicago.edu/founders/documents/a1_8_8s12.html .

Litman, Jessica. *Digital Copyright.* Amherst: Prometheus, 2001.

Madison, James. *Monopolies.* http://www.constitution.org/jm/18191213_monopolies.htm.

Nill, Alexander, and Andreas Jr. Geipel. "Sharing and Owning of Musical Works : Copyright Protection from a Societal Perspective." *Journal of Macromarketing* (Sage) 30, no. 1 (Novemeber 2010): 33-49.

Seadle, Michael. "Copyright in the networked world: the technology of enforcement." *Library Hi Tech* (Emerald) 26, no. 3 (2008): 498-504.

Sony Corp. v. Universal City Studios. 464 U.S. 417 (U.S. Supreme Court, January 17, 1984).

Rimmer, Matthew. *Digital Copyright and the Consumer Revolution: Hands Off My iPod.* 2007: Edward Elgar Publishing, 2007.

Afterword

On the Pirate Party

Rick Falkvinge

The pirate movement ultimately has the same origins as the green movement. It originated in the hippie ideas of challenging blind authority and putting everybody on equal footing, the ideas of sharing and caring - but unlike the green movement which could be carried by contemporary culture, the pirate movement had to hibernate in computer labs for 40 years until adoption of the prerequisite technology was widespread.

This was frequently referred to as "the hacker mentality": that knowledge, curiosity, sharing, and tinkering are never crimes. A genuine willingness to share knowledge and work unselfishly, in the comfort and experience that everybody benefits in the end if many enough people share. The hackers were intelligent, sensitive, rich in language nuance and playfulness, and defied all stereotypes of what a person of that age should be doing - they were playing games or sitting in the computer lab writing arcane code. This subculture grew and developed at universities like Stanford, MIT, and CalTech, far away from the spotlights of mainstream media.

Bill Gates wrote a famous column decrying this mentality early in his career, called "an open letter to hobbyists", where he essentially said that this mentality is harmful to business. Some 30 years later, Mr. Gates is one of the world's richest men, and the hacker mentality has taken a back seat to the ascent of corporate rule not just in this aspect, but in every aspect of our lives.

The backlash was inevitable.

Actually, the backlash had been growing in the underbrush for quite some time. When the Commodore 64 hit the homes in the early 1980s, games and other programs were mostly stored on tape cassettes - the same kind of tape cassette you'd use for music. Everybody had a so-called "double-decker" at the time: a music cassette player with two cassette slots, so that one cassette could play and the other record at the same time, making a copy in the process. Thus, seeing computer games and code stored on the exact same cassettes as music, the culture of copying and sharing among friends carried over immediately to the new environment of games and programs.

So copying and sharing among friends was not just socially accepted - it was socially expected.

This escalated further with the advent of so-called Bulletin Board Systems (BBSes) in the mid-1980s, which was essentially an amateur's internet that used phone lines to communicate. People would connect to remote BBSes, drop files there, and other people would collect them. Pretty much like we do today with file lockers, only at a much slower speed and with hard drives that were maybe 80 megabytes (!) in size. At this point, the mainstream press did the occasional scare story describing how asocial, aggressive individuals would further drift away from social behavior while being consumed by computer addiction. (Ourselves, we pretty much enjoyed discussing in the forums and mail boards that existed - pretty much like a forum today, only with a more primitive technology.)

Then, Napster hit in 1999.

From the mid-1990s onward, this thing called "internet" had been gradually rolled out commercially, replacing our previous amateur networks. We were not too happy about it initially, as it seemed mostly like another corporate glitz thing when we had a network we were happy with already. It didn't take long to scrape on the surface of the advertising and realize that the hacker mentality was alive and well in this other network as soon as you ditched the sales drones, and thus, most hacker types found themselves right at home in it.

In addition, Sweden was in a unique position at the time. In most parts of the world, the net had been rolled out by cable companies and telecom companies, which are the exact companies you don't want to see doing this: they have a very strong strategic incentive to make sure that the internet never takes off to its full potential, as that would destroy their existing business and sunk investments. (Why would I pay per minute for a 9.6-kilobit-per-second connection that can only be used for voice communications, when I have 100 megabits per second that can be used for anything at a fixed charge?) In contrast, the net was rolled out by private entrepreneurs in Sweden with no such baggage. They fibered up apartments at 10 megabits per second from 1997 onward, at a cost of about $25 per month (and those 10 megabits quickly became 100 at the same price).

That's when the corporate and social cultures collided heads-on. As Napster hit, boy, did people share. And Sweden was in a politically very interesting situation: as that kind of technology becomes available not just to geeks, but to everybody, it kick started the public discussion of how this technology can - and maybe even should - be used.

It is not a coincidence that the pirates first politicized in Sweden. The technology adoption by the public was just a little bit ahead on the bell curve at the time, and therefore, so was the associated political mindset. At the same time, the politicians were increasingly in the corporate mindset, that this technology was something dangerous.

We observe here that the mindset of sharing has become political, and associated with a positive, connected lifestyle.

The generation growing up today has a connected lifestyle that is being described as a problem by the old guard. They share, they know, they look up knowledge and culture, they verify statements at the source, and they trust no authority that demands to have its word taken for blind truth. No wonder there was - and is - a major clash with the current establishment.

In 2001, the copyright industry lobby established the Anti-Pirate Bureau in Sweden, intended to enforce the copyright monopoly and "educate" the public- an initiative taken at least 30 years too late. After two years of ridiculous statements from this lobby in mainstream media, a couple of culture activists decided to take the bull by the horns and founded a think tank of their own. In naming it, they wanted to assert that they were not against the future, but were the future. Thus, they were the Pirate Bureau (Piratbyrån).

The Pirate Bureau was an immediate smash hit with the media, explaining the hacker mentality of sharing, curiosity and freedoms of speech under the "pirate" banner - which, after all, was not chosen by them, but by their adversaries. Being a pirate became being a freedom fighter against corporate rule, and this discussion took place everywhere.

Everywhere but in the halls of legislation. The lobby roamed there undisturbed.

In 2005, three things happened that set me thinking. There was a fight about software patents in the European Parliament that we very narrowly lost, which would have essentially outlawed free software. There was yet another copyright monopoly harshening in Sweden, targeting the distribution channels of independent artists. And there was the Data Retention Directive, which turned our mobile phones into governmental tracking devices.

I realized that activism is not enough. Politicians needed to fear for their jobs, or they were not going to care. The issues needed to be politicized. But politics is a numbers game and a spectator sport; would there be votes in sufficient quantity?

There were 1.2 million file sharers in Sweden at the time, and if just one-fifth of them were tired enough of being constantly demonized by the politicians, then a new party would be in Parliament. The plan was sound. Yes, this plan could actually work.

Moreover, getting a tie-breaker position in Swedish parliament would be enough to turn Sweden; we would need just over 4% of the votes to win. With Sweden being part of the European Union, and the EU being a larger economy than the United States, trade sanctions would not be an effective response to reducing the monopolies. With resources from Swedish Parliament, we could then repeat the success in a few more key countries in Europe and turn Europe to the pirate perspective, and once the world's largest economy doesn't respect artificial scarcity, the rest of the world has no choice but to follow.

Sweden, Europe, and the world. In that order. This really could actually work, I thought.

So on January 1, 2006, I set up a web page at the domain piratpartiet.se - meaning "The Pirate Party". The name was copied from the Pirate Bureau, who had already established pirate policies in the Swedish mainstream media; tacking on the "party" meant that you could vote for those policies. After having mentioned the website in a chat channel once - just once - the whole thing detonated with activists who wanted to be a part of changing the world. 300 activists arrived on the very first day, and the new party became headlines all over the world. Other people started setting up similar initiatives in other countries right away.

But policies continued in the wrong direction. Politicians - and corporations - saw the diversity of thoughts, ideas, and people on the net as a threat, whereas pirates celebrated sharing, curiosity, diversity, and equalization. There was a complete clash of values.

The most striking theme of this new party was not about its policies, however, but on the meta-level: it changed how politics is made. It increased participation. The new format of politics required that everybody has the opportunity - and equal opportunity - to voice their opinion. This was something the old guard is not prepared for.

This, too, is a result of the connected lifestyle that the pirates defend. It has given everybody a voice. A 9-year-old schoolgirl in Paraguay now has the exact same strength of voice as a white middle-aged male in the rich parts of Europe, and the new generation celebrates that, and the diversity it brings. But the previous elite that used to set the narrative, that used to have the privilege of dictating the narrative, is horrified.

It's reasonable to ask why they are so horrified of the people that will replace them in 20 years.

After all, the new generation in terms of policy isn't demanding crazy things of rocket science. At their core, they are merely demanding the same civil liberties that applied to their parents in the offline world to carry over into their own lifestyle in the online world. That's a perfectly reasonable demand, and it doesn't matter whether those civil liberties mean that some old companies can't make money any more. No corporation gets the luxury of shaping society to guarantee them a profit; it goes the other way around - it is the job of every entrepreneur to make money given the current constraints of society and technology. They don't get to dismantle civil liberties, even if they can't make money otherwise.

With the verdict against the Pirate Bay being perceived as a grievous injustice just weeks before the European Elections in 2009, the Swedish Pirate Party's entry into the European Parliament was all but certain. At the same time, the Swedish Piratpartiet grew from 14,000 to 50,000 members.

So with Sweden's Piratpartiet having succeeded in a smashing proof-of-concept in the 2009 European Elections, where we got 25% of the below-30 vote and two out of Sweden's 20 seats in the European Parliament, Germany's *Piratenpartei* is now polling at consistent double digits. (It is important to note here that in European politics, if you take 10% of the votes, you get 10% of the seats. This is true for almost all countries in Europe.)

All of a sudden, we're much closer to our goal of winning Europe. The political balance for or against the net and civil liberties is precarious in Europe, with almost all of Eastern Europe - the part of Europe formerly behind the Iron Curtain - celebrating a tool that won't let governments suppress the citizenry, whereas the West sees it as a threat and wants it shut down, or at least censored and wiretapped. Winning Germany would mean that the pirate party movement tipped the scales of balance in political power in Europe in favor of the liberty-friendly faction, and that would mean that we would be approaching the endgame where we won.

And once we win Europe, we've won the world. We're well on our way.

falkvinge.net

'Because "Sharing is caring"…

fin